Lessons for Citizens of a New Democracy

Lessons for Citizens of a New Democracy

Peter C. Ordeshook

Professor of Government, California Institute of Technology, USA

THE SHAFTESBURY PAPERS, 10
SERIES EDITOR: CHARLES K. ROWLEY

Edward Elgar
Cheltenham, UK • Northampton, MA, USA

Published by
Edward Elgar Publishing Limited
8 Lansdown Place
Cheltenham
Glos GL50 2HU
UK

Edward Elgar Publishing, Inc.
6 Market Street
Northampton
Massachusetts 01060
USA

A catalogue record for this book
is available from the British Library

Library of Congress Cataloguing in Publication Data
Ordeshook, Peter C., 1942–
    Lessons for citizens of a new democracy / Peter C. Ordeshook.
    — (The Shaftesbury papers : 10)
    Includes bibliographical references and index.
    1. Democracy—Former Soviet republics. 2. Former Soviet
republics—Politics and government. I. Title. II. Series.
JC599.F607   1998
320.947'09'049—dc21
                                                          97–38257
                                                              CIP

ISBN 1 85898 545 5

Typeset by Manton Typesetters, 5–7 Eastfield Road, Louth, Lincolnshire LN11 7AJ, UK.
Printed and bound in Great Britain by Biddles Ltd, Guildford and King's Lynn

Contents

Acknowledgements		vi
1	Democracy: Just Another Experiment?	1
2	Must We Be Something Other Than What We Are?	8
3	Fools or Geniuses: What Are Voters Like In A Democracy?	15
4	Popular Referenda: Must We Vote to be Democratic?	22
5	What Is A Fair and Competitive Election?	28
6	Economics Or Politics: Which is the Chicken and Which the Egg?	35
7	Constitutional Rights: Mere Words or Sustainable Guarantees?	43
8	Democratic Institutions: Why Would They Influence Anything?	50
9	A New Constitution: Should We Cut Trees to Print It?	56
10	Constitutions: Are There Rules for How to Write Them?	63
11	Federalism: Ingredient for Stability or a Recipe For Dissolution?	69
12	Political Parties: A Source of Faction or Agents of Stability?	76
13	Legislatures: Can They Govern Us If They Cannot Govern Themselves?	83
14	A Two-Chamber Legislature: Isn't One More Than Enough?	89
15	Parliaments And Presidents: Legislative Incoherence versus Authoritarian Rule?	97
16	Emergency Clauses: Essential Precautions or A Lack of Faith?	103
17	Russia's Choices: An Accident Waiting to Happen?	111
18	Can We Be a Democracy?	121
Bibliography		127
Index		131

Acknowledgements

Originally written for an exclusively Russian audience and translated into Russian and updated to reflect contemporary events by Dr Vachyslav Nikonov (previously a deputy of the Russian Duma), approximately half of the essays in this volume were published between January and March 1993 in Moscow's *Nezavisimaya Gazeta* (*Independent Gazette*) under the editorship of Vitali Tretyakof when constitutional issues were at centre stage in Russian politics. Mr Tretyakof's courage and commitment to the ideal of Russian democracy cannot be understated and these essays would not have been written without his encouragement. Dr Nikonov (Slava) continues to educate me in the Russian perspective of things as he searches for ways to encourage the development of a stable democratic Russia. An extended version of Chapter 17 appeared in the April 1995 issue of *Journal of Democracy*. With respect to financial support of this project, I owe a special debt of gratitude to the University of Maryland's IRIS Program under the guidance and direction of Chris Clague and Mancur Olson, which generously supported the author in his 'meddling into Russia's internal affairs'. Finally, I would like to thank my colleague, Tom Schwartz, who helped me to develop as part of a larger project on constitutional design, many of the ideas offered here.

1. Democracy: Just Another Experiment?

Throughout the world, but especially in the successor states of the ex-USSR, citizens subsist with resignation and foreboding; draft constitutions are prepared, discussed, rejected, rewritten, ratified and amended; political leaders, mouthing patriotic slogans, follow the dictates of unrestrained personal ambition; public officials consolidate their power; optimistic economic projections yield little relief to the average person's plight; local currencies threaten to become each state's chief export, as wallpaper; crime runs rampant and becomes part of each state's structure; and executive and legislative branches contend for supremacy, while ethnic conflicts rage both within and without. As the pie shrinks, the self-serving fight harder for their piece, and citizens scramble for crumbs. The basis for pessimism is everywhere, and it is reasonable for people newly embarking on an experiment with democracy to respond with the plea, 'please ... no more experiments!'.

The demise of communist ideology confronts people everywhere with one of our most daunting and challenging tasks. New political institutions must be designed and set in place and new traditions of political discourse must be invented to guide the evolution of revolutionary economic relations at a time of severe economic dislocation. Although similar challenges may have confronted individual states one at a time, few eras in history have witnessed such sweeping changes that encompass such a diverse range of states. Russia is a continental power with a monstrously inefficient economy; Uzbekistan a destroyed ecology; Ukraine, with its artificial borders and ethnic, religious and linguistic divisions, threatens to disintegrate; and even the Baltic states have not wholly resolved who is a citizen and who is an unwanted 'guest'.

As daunting as the task appears, there are reasons for believing the challenge can be met. Many of the states striving for democracy possess a highly educated citizenry, a generously endowed geography and a rich cultural heritage, and others less well-endowed can anticipate some support from the rest of the world. There is the evident desire for just societies, and the recognition on the part of political élites that they must accommodate this desire or lose their grip on power. And there is the possibility of benefiting from the experiences of those states that have sought to move from autocratic to democratic rule. Some of these attempts have been successful; others have been otherwise. But those experiences, successful or not, offer valuable lessons for those who seek to establish stable and prosperous democratic governments today.

Democracy is no longer an experiment. More than two centuries have passed since the Americans began the 'experiment' with liberal constitutional democracy, and even longer since Britain began to teach the world something about constitutional restraint of the sovereign. And we have learned much since then. The study of politics is an imperfect science and no one argues that democracy can be begun easily in a society with an entrenched bureaucracy, with widespread economic deprivation, with rising ethnic tensions and with escalating rates of crime. But democracy can take root if individuals in society have the will to abide by its rules and if those rules are erected in accordance with some basic principles of political institutional design.

In this and the chapters that follow, we will survey the lessons democracy offers by its successes and failures. Setting these lessons in the context of current circumstances, we will proceed under the supposition that with but some nurturing and attention to proper matters, democracy and economic prosperity can prevail in Eastern Europe, Russia, Ukraine, Cuba and those other places that have suffered communist despotisms, as well as on those parts of the planet with traditions and cultures that have little experience with Western notions of democratic governance and individual rights.

We proceed on this venture because everyone who seeks to find their way in a new democratic state must become familiar with its operation, must understand what it is that democratic process can and cannot do, and must appreciate their responsibilities in it. The failure of any significant part of society to understand these things is the fertile ground upon which the potential despot sows his seed. We also address those with political ambition. Any significant failure to appreciate the role of constitutional limits, such as the sanctity of a free press (however personally uncomfortable that freedom might be), the necessity for upholding the rule of law even when adherence to it yields outcomes with which one disagrees, or the conflicts inherent in the colloquy of a free people, dooms a society to instability, ineffectiveness or despotism.

Just as people must learn the grammar of language to avoid being misled by those who would take advantage of their illiteracy, people must learn the grammar of democracy. Most of us learn language at an age when we are barely conscious of the fact of our learning. And although most of us cannot formally specify grammatical rules, we abide by those rules instinctively and leave formal understanding to linguists and teachers. So it is with the rules of democratic process. Few Americans, Costa Ricans, Swedes, Swiss or Germans can recite constitutional clauses, but these citizens possess an instinctive understanding of the rules of democratic process. In contrast, citizens of a new democracy must learn and adapt to a 'language' with which they are largely unfamiliar. And as with any new language, the initial stages of learning will result in innumerable errors and frustration.

Fortunately, democracy's 'grammatical rules' are not complex. But 'grammatical errors' here can be especially dangerous, so steps must be taken to minimize their occurrence. Part of the process of learning these rules is to understand what is of primary and what is of secondary concern. The things discussed most loudly or frequently are not always the most important. For example, although the relative power of a president versus a legislature is not unimportant, focusing on this issue alone can distract us from more fundamental concerns. Such debates often merely reflect a struggle among a small coterie of political élites and activists, so that only the struggle itself affects us – not its ultimate resolution. Political systems have survived and prospered with weak presidents (for example, Finland, Germany and Austria), with strong ones (for example, America and France) or with none at all (for example, Japan and Great Britain). Moreover, most systems have seen the powers of a president change with circumstances. America began with a constitutionally weak presidency that was soon transformed by those who held that office (Washington, Jackson and Lincoln); it entered its post Civil-War period in 1870 with a considerably weaker office that was transformed once again in this century by leaders such as Roosevelt, Johnson and Reagan.

We will not argue that the choice of presidential versus parliamentary government is an unimportant one. But we must learn when and why it is important – when it matters to us and when it matters only to those who compete for political position. Similarly, we must learn whether and how such things as a state's federal structure, its election laws and its representation formulas influence the provision of individual rights and political stability itself. What we want to accomplish here is to bring to the reader's attention what is of central importance in structuring the democratic state and what are merely derivative concerns. Of necessity, we will discuss such issues as: the advantages and disadvantages of presidential government; the rights a constitution can and cannot protect; alternative relationships between legislative and executive branches of government; the essential components of a federal state; the role of political parties in ameliorating conflict; and the influence on parties of alternative electoral procedures, designs of representative assemblies and federal relationships.

At times we will focus on details such as the advisability of constitutional emergency clauses, the organization of political parties and alternative voting procedures; at other times we will discuss more general things such as the obligations of democratic citizenship. However, in discussing such things we will try to show how these pieces fit together, how each is part of a general mosaic that determines the operation of a democratic state, and why it is generally impossible to discern the impact of one component of the design without assessing its function relative to all other components.

Our primary focus will be the institutional components of democracy – its constitution, election laws, legislative and executive prerogatives, and federal structures. This is as it should be, since the first rule of democratic design is:

Rule 1: All political processes – democratic and otherwise – proceed in accordance with rules, both implicit and explicit, constitutional and traditional. Building a democracy, then, is primarily a task of establishing new rules and new political institutions.

States beginning a journey to democracy do not require merely that they find the 'right leader' or implement precisely the 'right policy'. Patriotism is to be valued, and we prefer to avoid incompetent leadership or fool-hardy policy. But forming a stable democracy requires that we establish political institutions and traditions that will direct the actions of political leaders and society's citizens in the right way. In the democratic state, persons will be elected to high office with gross deficiencies of character and talent – democracy does not ensure perfection in our choices. But if our political institutions are well crafted, then the normal processes of the democratic state will compensate for such deficiencies.

But if institutions as opposed to mere personalities are to guide the democratic state, then it must also be the case that:

Rule 2: A democracy's primary institutional structures, especially those embodied by its constitution, must lie outside the control of any individual or oligarchy.

We cannot suppose that political élites will not try to subvert a democracy's rules and institutional structure for their own purposes – we should suppose that they will always search for ways to do so. However, the great trick of democratic design is to make that structure impervious to radical change by making the preservation of that structure in the self-interest of nearly everyone. Throughout this volume, then, we will try to trace the individual incentives that specific institutions create, including the incentive to maintain those institutions.

The experience of other states also tells us that the institutions of democracy come in many forms – there is no singularly perfect design. However:

Rule 3: Regardless of the structure ultimately agreed to, the parts of that structure must fit together so that the incentives they create are in balance.

Too often the legislative authority of the president, the basis of legislative representation, the rules of presidential selection, the relation of federal subjects to the national government, or the relation of ministers to the president versus the legislature, are negotiated in isolation from each other. The powers of the presidency are set to manipulate his authority over parliament, representation and election formulas are adopted with an eye to the strengths of contending groups, and federal relations and the role of ministers are negotiated as bargains between and among regional and national élites. However, none of these things can be discussed separately – a choice at one point affects the consequences of choices at all other points.

Because most transitions to democracy occur in a context of economic and political turmoil, it is tempting, when beginning the transition to democracy – when writing a new constitution – to try to resolve contemporary political conflicts directly through the design of society's new political institutions. But some separation between contemporaneous matters and longer-term concerns is essential. Specifically:

Rule 4: We should not suppose that society's inherent conflicts can be negotiated successfully at the time a democratic system of government is first designed and implemented.

Americans in 1787 negotiated two conflicts in their constitution: the power of large states versus small ones and the future of slavery. The first conflict soon became irrelevant and today we take little note of the fact that seemingly insignificant states such as New Hampshire or Delaware share equal representation in one branch of the legislature with California, which if an independent country, would place it in the top rank of global economies. And by attempting an artificial constitutional resolution of the second conflict without a clear constitutional resolution of the issue of secession, America set the stage for its Civil War – one of the bloodiest in history up to that time. Rule 4, then, can be restated thus:

> *Rule 5*: Those who would design a new democracy must focus on the institutional structures that will guide the resolution of whatever conflicts exist today and in the future with the understanding that the exact form of any resolution, as well as the nature of future conflicts, cannot be predicted with certainty.

Insofar as what we should expect of citizens themselves – the ultimate sovereigns in a democracy – citizens should be expected to favour politicians who espouse policies they perceive to be in their interest and to oppose (by legal means) those who advocate contrary measures. That is their right. Democracy's design should not be based on the supposition or requirement that citizens must become something other than what they already are. We do not commit the Marxist fallacy of supposing that our essential characters must somehow be reshaped. Nor should we suppose that political élites in a democracy will be motivated any less by self-interest than are the leaders of a despotism – the quest for power and control. Instead our task is to establish institutions so that those élites can pursue their self-interest in ways that serve our interests as well. Thus rather than search for leaders who argue that they have somehow subverted self-interest to the interest of society at large:

> *Rule 6*: We should judge political leaders primarily by their commitment to democratic process.

People should be prepared to support the politician, citizen, or organization that, even when advocating an unfavourable policy, does so in conformity with democratic practice, and to oppose those who proceed otherwise.

Much of what we have said may seem utopian, but our task will be to show that constructing a democracy in accordance with the rules we set forth here is not mere utopianism. These rules are more than mere exhortations. Few persons would have guessed that the citizens of Nazi Germany or Imperial Japan could accommodate democracy and the rules of governance imposed on them by victorious powers. But that is what they have done. Political institutions can be designed so that people will find it in their self-interest to act in accordance with these rules. Two hundred years ago, James Madison (*Federalist Papers*, no. 10) wrote in defence of the American constitution that, 'the seeds of faction are sown in the nature of man', and that, 'if men were angels, no government would be necessary'. Proceeding under these same assumptions keeps us from utopian fallacies and, with the success of other societies in mind, disallows undue pessimism.

2. Must We Be Something Other Than What We Are?

Citizens in a democracy are commonly told that they must meet special responsibilities to maintain their form of government: to be informed of public policy, to participate in democratic processes, to adopt special attitudes about the rights of others, and so on. But these admonitions are reminiscent of the ones articulated by a regime that sought to forge a communist utopia by breeding a new social consciousness. Thus such admonitions seem at odds with the argument of the previous chapter that democratic theory allows for the assumption that people cannot be perfected – that democratic institutions must be designed to operate in an environment in which people pursue a sometimes narrow self-interest, oblivious oftentimes to the social ramifications of their actions or the actions of others.

This apparent inconsistency demands resolution, especially in states that have lived under the yoke of communism. First, we do not want to endanger any transition to democracy by fostering the incorrect and dangerous belief that a radical transformation of the human psyche is an essential component of that transition. Second, we want to confront the oft-repeated assertion that 'democratic principles are alien to Country X's character', that 'X's political traditions preclude the possibility that its people can manage a democracy', and that 'only the strong leader can direct X's destiny'. Thus we ask: are there qualities that citizens of stable democracies possess that citizens of, say, the ex-Soviet Union do not? Is there any inherent reason for supposing that democracy cannot take root on territory once ruled by a communist despotism, or on the territory of anyone else not currently governed by a democratic state?

Our answer to such questions is no. However, our answer is not predicated on the supposition that people within any state or territory do not possess a unique character, traditions or culture that require special recognition. We predicate it on the argument that democracy does not demand that we be much different from what we are regardless of our traditions, language, religion, ethnicity, culture or what have you.

This is not to say that the smooth operation of democracy does not require that we think differently about individual rights and liberties and about the rule of law. Certainly it requires the gradual development of different expectations about the role of the state and about our relationship to it. We must believe that it is legitimate to oppose those who would tread on our rights, and certainly democracy works poorly when we do not respect the rights of others. But, as we hope to show, whatever differences are required are but slight adjustments in how *any* civilized society functions, and they come naturally if our political institutions are designed correctly.

To illustrate, consider the admonition that the citizens of a democracy should keep themselves informed of politics and of the actions of those who claim to represent them in national, regional or local legislatures. After all, ignorance, we are told, is the lever most commonly used by those who would subvert our freedoms. However, most of us have more immediate concerns than paying attention to the moves of politicians who may be thousands of miles distant – concerns that include feeding our families, securing our personal safety, maintaining our friendships, raising our children and earning a living. Moreover, being fully informed about politics is not only time-consuming, it can also appear fruitless. It is fruitless (even dangerous) in a dictatorship, but things do not always seem much better in a democracy. After all, few in a democracy can greatly affect political outcomes directly, if we can affect them at all. In voting for a president or even for a local representative, the likelihood that our vote is decisive for anything is infinitesimal. Thus in deciding how to invest our time, we are much more likely to invest it in those things we can control than in the distant matters of political process.

What we have just said applies everywhere. Few Americans know the name of their representatives, few Frenchmen know the organization of the European Economic Community, few Costa Ricans know the impact of their government's trade policies, and few Indians know the political composition of their national legislature. Indeed politics in most democracies seems little different than a sports event: people may cheer passionately for one team or another, but they know that there is little they can do individually to influence who wins or who loses. Or, to put matters differently, if given a choice between investing in learning about the details of government policy versus learning about, say, how to repair the plumbing of a broken sink, it is far better to invest in plumbing.

Still, democracies do function and we must ask: how can masses of people, preoccupied with things other than self-governance, self-govern? The answer lies in the extra-constitutional organizations that arise in a democracy (or precede its establishment): political parties, agricultural unions, political clubs, professional organizations, workers' groups, and the like. Democracy is something more than a great mass of citizen-voters and constitutionally proscribed institutions led by a few political élites. It consists also of a large number of subsidiary structures that arise to connect people to their government. These structures organize, lead and inform. They teach us essential facts. They guide our vote. And they provide the means whereby we can peacefully organize to protest against policies we deem unwise or opposed to our interest.

Such structures do not arise because people in a democracy are somehow different from those elsewhere. There is nothing in the water that gives Americans, Taiwanese, Indians, Mexicans or Costa Ricans any special advantage or that makes them more able than Ukrainians, Poles, Uzbeks or anyone else at creating these organizations. Russians are not perennially disadvantaged merely because eighty years ago a Czar prohibited meaningful political action, because such action was dangerous when the country was a despotism, or because Russia progressed along a different path of economic development than Western Europe. Instead the organizations that fill the gap between citizen-voters and constitutional institutions arise because those institutions can be influenced by concerted collective action. Because worker collectives, neighbourhood committees and social clubs can mobilize voters for and against political candidates, citizens can act through them to influence political outcomes. And when offered a menu of organizations in which to participate, people learn which serve their interests and which advocate contrary positions. Indeed it is often unnecessary for most people even to participate actively in such things – they can merely observe who it is that these organizations support and oppose. In this way, rather than becoming informed directly about candidates and their policies, people can learn from the actions of others.

For example, if a person is concerned about environmental policy and if there is a full range of interest groups seeking to influence such policy – some favouring the status quo, some favouring radical government regulation and still others sympathetic to the problems that confront the entrepreneur – then we can monitor the candidates that these groups support. In this way, these groups save us from the necessity of becoming fully informed about the details of policy or the sincerity of each candidate's utterances. Similarly, as workers or as farmers we may not know what policies are in our own self-interest. Will more government regulation protect me against unscrupulous business practices, or will it merely stifle investment that my country needs? Are budget deficits good because they allow the government to invest in infrastructure or do they merely lead to inflation? Once again, the average citizen cannot be expected to answer such questions, especially when the 'experts' themselves disagree. But he can get some guidance from his labour union, farm collective, agricultural association, or even social club about which candidates are likely to be sympathetic to his interests.

A good example of this process is America's Association for Retired People (AARP), which is a privately organized entity that monitors public retirement and medical care programmes and informs its members about the positions of politicians on these issues. It is almost certainly one of the (if not *the*) most influential interest groups in the United States. The elderly not only care greatly about such issues, but they also stand ready to support or oppose political candidates with their votes. Thus with millions of members (anyone above the age of 55 can join for a modest annual fee), the politician who earns the ire of this association does so at his or her peril. In summary, then, the AARP monitors the behaviour of all relevant politicians and holds a reputation of providing reasonably accurate information; the elderly rely for their information about politicians on the AARP's publications; and, completing the circle, politicians are loth to advocate or to vote for policies that are not in the interest of the elderly, because they know that their actions are being watched.

Of course, it may seem unexceptional that entities such as the AARP arise in 'mature democracies' with traditions of citizen political organization and participation. What we must explain is why we anticipate the emergence of such things in countries only now making the transition to democracy. The process we are describing is not perfect and people will not be misled by it only if there is an effective (competitive) market-place for political ideas. And we cannot exclude the possibility that political leaders will seek to exert authoritarian control over this market-place when it is in their interests to do so. We cannot assume that those in power will not try whenever possible to preclude the existence of those things and activities that might threaten their position. There are two protections against this possibility, each of which depends on the other and neither of which imposes special requirements on culture or tradition. The first condition should be self-evident: a free and unfettered press. However democratic a political system might appear, if the state controls the activities of the press – even if it is for the well-intentioned purpose of ensuring fair coverage of political events – then history teaches an unambiguous lesson:

> *Rule 7*: Those in positions of governmental authority are incapable of resisting the temptation to have the media operate for their benefit. And if the media operate primarily for the benefit of those in power, then we are soon deprived of the right and the ability to organize, to uncover, and to oppose the deceptions that political élites will attempt.

It is essential, then, that constitutions contain an unambiguous and unqualified guarantee of press freedom. However, this guarantee is nothing more than words on parchment unless it is accompanied by something else: competitive elections. If democracy has one essential characteristic, it is the power of citizens to replace one set of leaders with another:

> *Rule 8*: The thing that distinguishes democracy from other forms of government is its basic premise that the ultimate sovereign is the people and that their ultimate right of sovereignty is the right to choose their political leaders. Hence without competitive elections, nothing else matters.

The difficulty is that if competitive elections require a free press and if a free press requires competitive elections, what guarantees that both protections are sustained? A more complete answer to this question must await subsequent chapters of this volume. Here we note simply that it is within the cauldron of competitive elections that many, if not most, of the organizations arise that allow citizens to become informed, to mobilize politically and, ultimately, to defend their rights, including the right to a free press. The elements of a civil society do not arise like mushrooms in a forest merely because citizens seek to influence politicians. They arise and are sustained out of the self-interest of politicians. They arise in large part because one set of politicians seeks to defeat some other set, and because politicians have an incentive to engineer and support the organizations they think will support them. It might seem that politicians would find the existence of organizations such as the AARP discomforting. Who appreciates having someone looking over one's shoulder, waiting to broadcast mistakes to anyone who will listen? But politicians can also welcome such things, since they are often the vehicles they use to defeat an incumbent or to retain office once it is secured. Just as citizens require organizations of various types to help them exert their sovereign rights, politicians need those same organizations to secure their private ends (including campaign contributions).

Thus the complex social structures that characterize a mature democracy serve a dual purpose: they help citizens to organize for political action and they assist politicians in their careers. Out of this symbiotic relationship and within the context of competitive elections comes the protection of the right to organize, the right to possess information and the right to disseminate that information. People in a democracy do not rely for the preservation of their liberties on finding honourable, fair or just political leaders. They seek instead to devise institutions that will make acting honourably, fairly, and so on in the self-interest of those whom they elect to office.

Unlike democracy's formal structure – the powers of a president, election laws, and so on – the building blocks of a civil society cannot be planned. The government cannot decree the existence of citizen action groups and industrial lobbies. As we have already noted, they arise 'naturally' out of the market-place of democratic process. As a consequence, their precise character is as much a function of society's culture and traditions as anything else. Thus we do not expect the same social structures to arise in, say, Taiwan as in the United States, nor do we expect organizations with similar names to act the same way across societies. There may be similarities, but there will also be differences which those outside of a culture may find difficult to comprehend. However, regardless of the society in question and regardless of the details of these organizations, they will all serve the same general dual purposes of informing and organizing citizens for political action and facilitating the private goals of public officials.

Returning, then, to the question that forms the title of this chapter, we see no reason to argue that people must become something other than what they are in order to make a successful transition to democracy. There will be changes. Not all beliefs will remain constant, and people will learn to hold different attitudes towards their government and towards each other. People will come to expect politicians to be responsive to their needs, and they will grow accustomed to seeing their fellow citizens pursuing their ends through politics. But just as the economic market produces the 'right' number of bicycles, cabbage graters and screwdrivers, the political market-place of a functioning democracy produces the 'right' amount of political information and activism. There may be 'market failures', as when political élites use the power of the state to hide their misdeeds. But if political institutions are well designed, those misdeeds will be discovered eventually or they will be of minimal consequence to the rest of us. Of course, there is no guarantee of perfection. But if there is a difference between democracy and communism it was communism's supposition that it could, through planning or brute force, change traditions and values as well as human nature; democracy requires no such assumption.

3. Fools or Geniuses: What Are Voters Like In A Democracy?

Suppose a new constitution has been adopted, that new elections are scheduled and that candidates from the Right and Left are emerging to press their arguments for your support. In ex-communist states some of them are *apparatchiks* proclaiming that only they understand 'the system' and can make it work; others are technocrats who argue that they have discovered truth and are uncorrupted by a system we should all forget; others proclaim a need to return to 'past glories' with the argument that the current spate of leaders has merely betrayed society's principles; and still others, when ethnic divisions are present, talk only of the necessity for correcting past injustices. Political parties proliferate like weeds, each with the word 'Democratic', 'People', 'Worker', 'Progressive' or 'Liberal' in its name and each with a formal membership small enough to fit in your kitchen. Candidates promise instant solutions, while proclaiming their honesty, and devotion to family and to country. And there you sit, trying to decide what to think, how to vote and whether to give a damn.

The fear is that voters, out of apathy or ignorance, will elect candidates who will promulgate ill-conceived economic policies, who will merely provide ineffective leadership or who will ride to victory on divisive ethnic or nationalistic appeals. How can voters make sense of this rhetoric and act reasonably? How can one be certain that others will not act unreasonably, so that the only protection is to abide by a counter-balancing extremism?

Such questions have no simple answer. Democracy, as we said earlier, comes without guarantees, including one against our own folly. However, despite the centuries of despotic rule experienced by most of the world, there is no reason to suppose that voters in one country will act much differently to those elsewhere. If there are differences, they lie in the political institutions that direct the self-interest of people and their leaders, in combination with the pre-existing interests of people as determined by economic and social structures. And so, to gauge how people in Russia, Ukraine, Cuba or China might respond to similar institutions, let us look at how voters act in established democracies, both new and old. We begin with three myths about voters. First:

> *Myth 1*: After carefully studying the issues and candidates, voters in a democracy cast their ballots for whoever best serves their interest.

Few people believe this myth, for the simple reason that it cannot be true. As we argued in the previous chapter, most voters have better things to do than study politics. Given that a single vote is unlikely to change anything, it is more reasonable for people to learn about things they can influence – how to earn some extra income or where to go in search of lower prices. Most people accept a myth of the opposite sort, namely:

> *Myth 2*: Voters in most democracies are easily baffled by meaningless campaign promises. Confused by politics, they vote for the candidate with the best smile, the most money or the most emotionally satisfying appeal. In this way democracies, especially new ones, become vulnerable to dangerous demagogues and vile extremists.

But this myth is no more true than the first. Some voters will search for extreme solutions if they think 'the system' has failed – voters everywhere can believe for a time that there are simple solutions to complex problems or that only the existence of 'evil forces' explains their plight. But just as voters are not genius policy analysts, they are not fools. People may be poor or incompletely educated, but they are not necessarily more stupid than anyone else. Voters everywhere make mistakes, but often on the basis of criteria that make it obvious that they have acted unwisely only after the fact.

Some commentators might argue that the rise of an extremist such as Vladimir Zhirinovsky in Russia is a counter-example to our argument. How else can we understand an electorate that supports his preposterous promises and inflammatory rhetoric? But Zhirinovsky did not materialize and win votes because Russian voters are stupid, ill-informed or more nationalistic than voters elsewhere. Instead we can trace his success to stupidity on the part of those 'democratic reformers' who thought that the correctness of their policies should be self-evident to all but unrepentant communists; of those who, like Boris Yeltsin, thought it possible to maintain a Czar-like distance from electoral processes; of those who were more concerned with advancing their own careers than anything else; or of those who believed that voters were sheep, easily led by a broadcast media controlled by the state.

A third myth is less a myth than a misunderstanding of the importance of things. That myth is:

Myth 3: Money is the only important thing and elections are won by whoever spends the most.

Money is anything but unimportant – for good reason it has been proclaimed the 'mother's milk of politics'. But while it is critical in determining a candidate's ability to attract voters, a candidate must first *have* a message and voters must be susceptible to receiving it. If voters are satisfied, even well-financed challengers face difficult prospects; if voters are dissatisfied, a challenger can be victorious even if outspent.

Voters in stable democracies do make reasonable decisions by relying on three relatively accessible sources of information. The first is their personal experience. If voters believe that their welfare has improved and will continue to do so, they tend to vote for incumbents; otherwise they search for alternatives. A voter's second source of information are the opinions of friends or of people and, as we outlined in the previous chapter, organizations he or she trusts. People operate with the reasonable assumption that by looking at the experiences of those in similar circumstances, they gain a better sense of a government's competence.

Naturally, what we have said refers only to tendencies. Candidates must still find ways to mobilize people who are largely disinterested in politics. That 'way' is the voter's third source of information – the political party. Political parties in a new democracy do not always form, of course, to mobilize voters and to elect candidates. Some are merely ways for specific individuals to secure public visibility. Others are mere protest groups formed around a single issue, and are organizationally unsuited to compete in an election. And still others are remnants of alliances that sought to overthrow an old regime. When such alliances disintegrate (which they commonly do since their members often have little in common other than opposition to a regime), the fragments, for lack of a better label, call themselves parties.

Regardless of their genesis, parties are universal fixtures of democracies for two reasons, one having to do with voters and the other with candidates. First, parties are the link between political activists and the great mass of people for whom politics is often little more than a spectator sport. They give voters their voice through the ballot box in a normally functioning democracy, or they spur them to more violent action in an abnormally functioning one. In stable democracies, however, parties do more. Voters need a way to give structure to their political information and experiences. Party labels, much like the sections of a filing cabinet, are such a device. Using these labels, voters learn which parties are responsible and which nominate candidates that serve their interests. Over time, they begin to identify with specific parties and vote for them or their candidates unless presented with a compelling reason to act otherwise – scandal, economic depression, the mishandling of an international crisis. In fact, party identifications can become so strong that, even when compelled to defect, a voter will do so only temporarily.

Party labels, then, are the device whereby voters organize the incoherent political information to which they are subjected before, during and after an election. Politicians soon learn that success requires being associated with something other than a social club or protest group. A stable democracy cannot remain in a situation in which countless parties manoeuvre for position, constantly divide, subdivide, recombine and change labels. If a democracy survives, the parties that survive with it are those that establish brand labels for themselves like the brand labels of consumer products. People eat at MacDonald's or purchase Japanese electronics because of their reputation for quality or efficiency; people support parties that succeed in associating desirable policies, philosophies and candidates with their labels.

But now the imperatives of electoral competition exert two pressures on parties. The first leads them to consolidate; the second dictates the form of this consolidation. Because parties must try to establish brand labels, they must show some initial successes and they must grow and compete for a broader range of public offices. This leads some parties with similar philosophies to combine under the same label in much the same way as companies with similar products competing in different markets combine to take advantage of their mutual strengths.

Here, though, the form of consolidation depends on whether the political system is parliamentary or presidential. In a parliamentary system, a party's first priority is to secure legislative representation and to participate in the formation of a government. Party leaders may be satisfied with controlling only a few seats, especially if compromising their positions in the quest for greater representation only causes them to lose the support they originally enjoyed. Whatever forces operate to cause consolidation among parties will be further attenuated to the extent that parliamentary deputies are elected by party-list proportional representation (PR), as opposed to the single-member district election schemes associated with the United States, Britain, Canada and Australia, since PR allows even small parties to participate in legislative deliberations. Thus parliamentary government – especially one with PR – will commonly be characterized by a number of parties scattered across the political spectrum.

In presidential systems – in systems with a relatively powerful and directly elected chief of state – parties must focus on the main prize, the presidency, and they must consolidate further to win. Voters, in fact, lose interest in those that have no chance of winning the presidency. Few persons want to waste their vote by casting it for someone who cannot be anything but a footnote in a history book. Thus the actions of voters alone tend to eliminate small parties in presidential systems. This consolidation, in turn, will draw the surviving parties towards the centre of opinion on most issues rather than leaving them, as in a parliamentary system, scattered across the landscape. If parties on either the Right or Left fail to coalesce, then their opposite number can win the presidency by doing so. And if they coalesce at the extremes, then the party closest to the centre of opinion wins. In the long run, then, neither side can resist failing to consolidate under only a few brand labels near the centre of public opinion on salient issues.

Of course, consolidation and convergence take time, and if anything can derail this process it is ethnicity and nationalism. Indeed if there is a fear that the citizens of a democracy can act emotionally or dangerously, it is when we talk of ethnicity or its correlates – language and religion. But in judging how a democracy can contend with such issues, we should begin with the fact that if politicians seek one thing it is issues that work to their advantage, that mobilize voters to their side. Some candidates appeal to class, others to urban–rural conflicts, some try to gain entry by championing environmental matters and some take up the cause of pensioners, workers, and so on. In stable democracies, this search accounts for nearly all domestic legislation and new governmental programmes. Unfortunately, ethnicity and its dual, nationalism, are too obvious for politicians to ignore. And if ethnicity correlates with territoriality and class, then the contours of political competition become steep and dangerous.

In assessing how a political system and the voters in it are likely to respond to such issues, we must learn how parties are likely to respond.

Will ethnicity cause parties to splinter or to become more radical, or can they absorb and blunt ethnic and nationalist agitation? We can answer this question by first noting another myth of democracy:

Myth 4: Under majority rule, a majority will control the state to the detriment of any minority.

Of course, Myth 4 need not be a myth at all. But Myth 4 has proven itself to be otherwise not because people were somehow evil, ill-informed or undemocratic by nature, but because those systems were designed to ensure such control through manipulations that rendered their political system anything but democratic. In contrast, in a well-designed democracy, parties or governmental coalitions are compelled, through a variety of institutional devices, to compete at the margin for minority support. In their search for ways to form or maintain winning coalitions, parties and politicians in stable democracies have incentives to attract the support of all ethnic groups and thereby to facilitate internal resolutions of ethnic conflicts.

We cannot understate the importance of co-optation. Martin Luther King succeeded in the United States without creating instability: rather than militant opposition, he advocated the extension of constitutional rights to blacks while offering political support to both the Democratic and Republican parties. Both parties, as a product of the competition between them, responded by passing the civil rights legislation of the 1960s, which in turn blunted the appeal of militant leaders. King anticipated this response – he anticipated that, although both black and white extremists would oppose him, 'the white establishment', acting in its own self-interest, would support him. Peaceful non-violent resistance, then, was more than mere ideological conviction – it was part of a strategy that induced the major parties to give him what he wanted. In this way, King's strategy, as leader of a minority, was not to protest the basic majoritarian form of US politics; rather it was to make himself pivotal between the two political parties that competed within the majority.

One can object that this scenario applies only to established democracies. In states with weaker traditions of democratic governance, different groups will believe that past injustices ought to be corrected immediately, and that the only correction is secession, independence or even bloodshed. This will be especially true among groups that have never experienced democracy and that have little reason to believe that opponents will abide by democratic process. Ethnic conflicts, however, are rarely spontaneous events. They have causes that can be treated with such devices as a decentralized federal system that invests regional and local governments with real power, a national legislative chamber that gives coalitions of federal subjects a veto over legislation, and electoral laws that remove the incentives for political élites to appeal to baser human instincts when searching for political support. Just as few voters gather detailed information about normal politics, few will act to secede or instigate violence unilaterally. Secession and violence must be organized. Thus the great trick of political institutional design in an ethnically heterogeneous state is to establish institutions that give political parties an incentive to co-opt ethnic leaders so that they can pursue their objectives within established structures.

This incentive to co-opt will, as we have already noted, arise naturally among national parties seeking to form winning coalitions. But this incentive can be re-enforced by noting that just as a society's majority is rarely homogeneous, minorities are not either (unless, through overt isolation and discrimination, ethnicity correlates with all other issues). Heterogeneity, in turn, opens the door to political competition within ethnic groups. And since the different sides to that competition will seek allies at the national and local political levels, the door is open as well to national and local parties that will try to extend their coalitions to these different ethnic groups and nationalities. Local political competition, then, should be encouraged, which is best done by ensuring that governments control real and valued resources and by allowing the citizens of those governments to direct the distribution and use of the resources. So democratic reform that encourages competition must do so at all levels of government, not just at the national level. Stating an argument that we will repeat frequently throughout this volume, the danger of democratic transition is often not too much but too little democratic reform. Reform must give local political leaders an opportunity to compete, it must give them an avenue to participate in national organizations, and it must give national leaders incentives to encourage this participation. If 'reform' does otherwise, the connection between national parties and ethnic minorities is destroyed. And once this occurs, political extremists will be only too happy to fill the void and mobilize people to political action of a different sort.

4. Popular Referenda: Must We Vote to be Democratic?

As charges and counter-charges of dictatorship, irresponsibility and simple stupidity filled the air early in 1993 in Russia's People's Congress, the only solution to the apparent paralysis of politics seemed to be to 'go to the people'. Let the people speak – hold a referendum! But what question would voters be asked? Will it be 'Should Russia be ruled by a president or the parliament?' or 'Should the Congress have the right to fire members of the president's cabinet?' or 'Should the Congress be dissolved and forced to confront new elections?' or 'Should there be a new presidential election?' or 'Should there be new elections to choose *everybody*?' or 'Does Russia need a new constitution?' or 'Should the constitution provide for a strong or weak president?' Russia held its vote, and although the returns gave Yeltsin a reason to argue that he enjoyed a mandate to lead, opponents used those same returns to claim the opposite. The referendum resolved little and only prefaced the eventual dissolution of Russia's parliament later that year.

Despite such events (not to mention Gorbachev's ill-fated referendum on the survival of the Soviet Union itself), referenda are viewed as an important part of democracy. Complexity may require that we write law through representative intermediaries – parliaments, presidents, ministers and governmental bureaucrats. But, the argument continues, because elected officials can be insensitive to, or can misinterpret, public needs, it is best to consult the public directly on important matters. Once a seemingly clear expression of the popular will is revealed, who in a democracy dares resist that will – who prefers to be labelled 'anti-democratic' or 'authoritarian'? Who could oppose a referendum's conclusion (except in those instances in which the referendum itself is worded so as to preclude anything but a single outcome, as was the case with Gorbachev's referendum)?

It is important, however, to have a realistic understanding of the use and misuses of referenda and of voting generally. This is especially true since, when we look closely at the assumptions that underlie a referendum's presumed legitimacy, we find three assumptions that cannot be sustained generally – assumptions that, continuing with the list we began in the previous essay, we can label as myths. The first assumption is:

Myth 5: Even if we exclude those who don't care or don't know, a popular will exists.

The next myth about referenda in a democracy is:

Myth 6: A referendum is the most straightforward way to reveal the popular will.

From these two myths we can infer a third, namely:

Myth 7: A referendum is 'more democratic' than other forms of voting in a democracy.

A healthy respect for public opinion is essential in a democracy. But none of these myths, which try to justify an exalted position for referenda, is universally valid. Consider the existence of a popular will, Myth 5. Certainly this will exists if preferences are unanimous. But in this instance there is rarely a need to learn it through referenda; no balloting is required to justify the supposition, for example, that a prosperous and stable society is a socially desirable outcome. So suppose we want to learn the popular will when preferences are not self-evident and unanimous. In this instance we need a rule with which to define that will, and the most generally accepted rule is majority rule. We appreciate that we might not always be willing to abide by this rule. Because we should not want to violate anyone's constitutional rights merely because a majority prefers to do so, most constitutions make the adoption of constitutional amendments a difficult undertaking even if a majority prefers change.

Suppose, however, that we confront an issue in which people agree that majority rule is appropriate. Thus if policy A is preferred by a majority to policy B, then A ought to be chosen over B. However, not all issues can be reduced to two alternatives. Those who would draft a new constitution, for example, do not confront a simple choice between a strong president versus a strong parliament – there are many ways to form the relationship between the different branches of government. Moreover, the issue confronting people when moving to democracy is not simply whether to hold elections today or sometime in the future. They must also decide the form of those elections, the form of the legislature and the relationship of the national government to the different components of local and regional governments.

What we want to show now is that whenever there are more than two alternatives, we encounter problems in reaching a definitive determination of the 'public will'. Suppose a majority prefers policy A to B, and a majority prefers B to some third policy, C. It appears that A ought to be selected. But notice that we have said nothing about the relationship between A and C. Since A is preferred to B and B to C, we might infer that A is preferred to C. But this need not be so. For example, suppose: (1) A calls for new legislative elections and postponement of a presidential election; (2) B calls for no elections whatsoever; and (3) C allows the current parliament to continue, and requires that a new president be elected by that parliament. Suppose the president's supporters prefer A to B to C; suppose those who are fearful of what new elections might bring but who are dissatisfied with the policies of the current president prefer B to C to A; and suppose that those who are disgusted with everyone, but especially with a parliament elected under the rules of a previous regime (a situation not uncommon to several of the successor states of the USSR), prefer C to A to B. Notice now that if each of these groups is equally numerous, then A is preferred to B by a majority, B is preferred to C by a majority, and yet C is preferred by a majority to A.

This example is important for several reasons, the most important being that, since A, B and C are each defeated in a majority vote by something, there is no popular will to be discovered. Nothing stands highest in society's preferences and nothing can lay unambiguous claim to being 'socially preferred'. Hence the first myth that justifies the legitimacy of referenda in terms of their ability to discover the popular will cannot be valid in all circumstances.

Our example also reveals Myth 6 as a myth: instead of revealing a popular will, referenda can manufacture that will and give politicians the opportunity to manipulate events. Since a referendum usually allows a choice between only two alternatives – most are framed in yes-or-no form – the final outcome in our example is determined wholly by which two alternatives are considered. If the referendum reads: 'Should a new presidential election be held?' (A versus C), the outcome is C. If the referendum reads: 'Should new parliamentary elections be held?' (B versus C), the outcome is B. And if the referendum reads: 'Should the president or the parliament be subject to new elections?' (A versus B), the outcome is A. Thus even if there is no popular will to be discovered, it can be 'manufactured' and manipulated by those politicians who can frame the questions the rest of us are expected to answer.

This critique of referenda does not employ any assumption about the inability of voters to hold informed opinions. People may be misinformed or misled, but our concern with referenda is that even with a fully informed electorate, they can give a false picture of things. They can lead us to think that there is a popular desire to move in one direction when there is no agreement whatsoever about things.

In fact, contrary to Myth 7, voting in a democracy plays a role other than allowing the public to determine policy directly, and it is an error to equate democracy with any such device. So to see voting's role and to discover democracy's essential character, let us consider representative democracy, the thing referenda are intended to supplant. Suppose our elected representatives (legislators, presidents, governors) are somehow sensitive to the preferences of those they represent. If there is no popular will, they should learn this fact. Indeed they will have incentives to do precisely that, out of fear that their election opponents will take advantage of their ignorance. Politicians also have an incentive to learn something referenda cannot reveal: the intensity of preferences. In this way, they will be in a better position to invent new alternatives, to weight differences in intensity, to evaluate the 'fairness' of different policies and to negotiate compromises. Of course, they will not necessarily do this out of good-will – they will do it to preserve their positions.

This is not to say that all legislatures can do these things. Members of a legislature that pre-dates full democracy are unlikely to have adjusted their thinking to the imperatives of competitive elections – they may have no idea what those imperatives are. We suspect, however, that parliamentary confusion in newly formed democracies reflects the absence of a well-defined public will as much as anything else. Although the early parliaments of most states formed out of the Soviet Union suffered from the malady of not being wholly democratically elected and from not being threatened with the prospect of competitive elections, they suffered also from the malady of trying to represent a population with incoherent preferences. Most persons agreed that the circumstances that prevailed after the fall of communism were unacceptable – everyone wanted a stable currency, a prosperous economy, a guarantee of individual rights and some certainty that the state would continue to provide a minimum of social welfare entitlements. But what was the 'popular will' with respect to the policies that must be implemented to achieve these ends? Because there did not exist (and still does not exist in some countries) any consensus on means, the conflicts within a legislature, as well as between the legislature and other political leaders, merely reflected society's divisions. A referendum alone could not resolve these matters.

With this argument we can now begin to see the role of voting in a democracy. Put simply, voting is the device the people use to choose their leaders, to choose those who they think represent their positions and preferences most effectively, and to replace those who they do not think have performed their jobs well:

> *Rule 9*: Political systems that allow the people to change their leaders through competitive elections are democracies – all other systems are something else. A system that allows people to decide things by referenda – even important things – but that relegates the design of those referenda and all other decisions to an unelected élite is not a democracy.

Thus the answer to the question that forms the title of this chapter is yes. But our answer does not require voting on referenda. In evaluating a constitution, we should not focus on the opportunities it provides for deciding issues directly or on the power it gives a president or a legislature to call plebiscites. These things may influence the relative power of different parts of a government, but they do not always impact the power of the voters themselves. Of greater importance in determining the responsiveness of public officials to the people are guarantees of meaningful and competitive elections. Will elections be held with sufficient frequency? Who controls the rules under which elections are held (we should be certain that they are not controlled by those who are directly governed by those rules, lest they manipulate them to their own advantage)? What direct and indirect measures does a constitution contain to ensure that elections will be competitive (does the constitution offer promises of campaign funds that a majority party can manipulate)?

None of this means that we see no role for referenda. Referenda are important devices for bringing issues to the attention of voters or for building a consensus among decision-makers over what direction to move policy, and, if used properly, they can offer voters a way to constrain the actions of politicians and other public officials. For example, voters in Switzerland can veto legislation that affects their taxes. In local elections in the United States, voter approval may be required before officials are allowed to increase public indebtedness. And referenda – initiatives – that can be instigated by voters themselves can spur otherwise recalcitrant legislators to action. Nevertheless, the key feature of these examples is that referenda are only a part of the political process. Because they are something more than a public opinion poll, voters might have an incentive to become better informed when voting in a referendum. Referenda, moreover, can direct politicians to exert greater efforts at resolving an issue, as when voters reveal that they are against secession or in favour of something else. However, referenda should not be interpreted as a substitute for the power of voters to decide who shall lead or represent them. Referenda are merely an auxiliary control and not the key element of a democracy.

5. What Is A Fair and Competitive Election?

Throughout its history, the Soviet Union required that its citizens march to the polls so it could announce that the victorious (and only) candidate had won with a turnout exceeding 99 per cent. A failure to vote resulted in a knock at the door and a demand that a ballot be filled in. In this way Andrei Vyshinsky could assert in 1937 that, 'never in a single country did the people manifest such activity in elections as did the Soviet people. Never has any capitalist country known nor can it know such a high percentage of those participating in voting as did the USSR'. The democratic world laughed derisively, and brushed aside the assertion of democratic legitimacy and superiority. However, although we may think we know an unfair or uncompetitive election when we see it, can we recognize its opposite? Must all candidates or parties have an equal chance of winning? Must all candidates have equal access to the media? Must the media be unbiased? Must all parties have equal financing? Must turnout exceed 50 per cent? Must political candidates refrain from criticizing each other with personal attacks? Must political parties represent a cross-section of society, mirroring its ethnic, linguistic and cultural diversity? And must there always be more candidates than there are offices to be filled?

The meaning of *fair and competitive* has changed much over time – so much so that there need not be general agreement about the content of this idea. 'Democracy' began in the 18th and 19th centuries with property requirements that kept most people from voting. Elections that excluded the participation of women were deemed fair in most of the world until World War I and until only recently in Switzerland, as were elections that did the same to blacks in America and Indians in Latin America. Elections in which incumbent politicians enjoy as much as 100:1 advantage in financing are commonplace today throughout the world's democracies. And elections that keep certain philosophies from being represented at the polls – separatist movements, religious movements, racist ones and ideological ones – are often regarded as otherwise fair and competitive (witness the German prohibition of Nazi agitation and the nearly equivalent American prohibition of anything that hints at the possibility that blacks are in any way inferior to whites).

Despite this history, we worry about perceptions of fairness, because if candidates believe that elections are unfair or uncompetitive, then they and their followers are less likely to operate under democratic rules and more likely to prefer unconstitutional actions. And if this view is widely held, then the legitimacy of the entire system is undermined and people become more acceptant of the demagogue. Unlike a regime that used elections to register solidarity with a Communist Party, elections are the means whereby the people exercise their sovereign right to replace one set of leaders with another – the right to 'throw the bums out'. Stripped of this right, democracy becomes a sham. Stripped of the belief that elections are fair, the stability of the political system becomes dependent wholly on its ability to coerce. Of course, since societies have prospered and been stable under a variety of definitions of fairness and competitiveness, the question we should ask is: what definition is appropriate today – what standards facilitate a stable democratic regime in the 20th and 21st centuries?

Naturally there are some criteria over which there is universal or near universal agreement:

Rule 10: No one above the age of responsibility should be denied the right to vote or should confront excessive obstacles to voting. It is tempting to want to exclude those 'judged incompetent by the court'. Who, after all, wants public policy decided by 'incompetents'? But the excesses to which this dangerous idea can be extended were only too clearly illustrated in the Soviet Union. And even if we assume that courts operate honestly, we need not prohibit incompetents from voting: if they are truly incompetent, they are unlikely to move an election from one candidate or party to another; and their number will be too small to matter in any electorate we can imagine.

Rule 11: Only voters should judge a candidate's qualifications. Let the anti-semite, fascist and unrepentant communist campaign. Once we allow some élite to enforce its judgements about seditious, inflammatory or immoral candidacies, or to deem certain parties illegal, democracy is compromised. The people can dispense with extremists by not supporting them.

Rule 12: New parties and candidates should be allowed to enter an election relatively freely. Just as the threat of competition keeps a firm from charging a monopoly price, the threat of competition compels those in power to work for the interests of society. Of course, just as every manufacturer prefers to be a monopolist, every politician prefers that no one contests his right to govern. But once the right of free entry is compromised, all other rights are jeopardized.

Rule 13: Elections should not be judged invalid if a candidate is unchallenged. Although the absence of a challenger might imply coercion, if all other requirements for a fair and competitive election are satisfied, the absence of a challenger may imply nothing more than the existence of a singularly popular candidate.

Rule 14: The media must have the right to publish any opinion regarding a candidate's qualifications and a party's activities. Public officials will try to use the power of their office to protect themselves from opposition. Allowing incumbents to wrap themselves in the protective cloak of official position precludes the possibility of fair and competitive elections. A wholly free press, able to investigate and report on the failings and accomplishments of incumbents and challengers alike, is essential.

Rule 15: No area of policy should be set off-limits for debate. All manner of issues should be subject to scrutiny, and the only criteria for their selection should be the electorate's willingness to listen to those who campaign on them. With an official gatekeeper of legitimate debate – a role despots and those who cannot comprehend democracy think only they should fill – the election is not unlike one in which the government controls the media.

Rule 16: Voters should be free from coercion and the voting booth should be off-limits to candidates and their supporters. In the long run, we would hope to see the formation of organizations whose express purpose is to oversee the honesty of voting procedures and whose charter is explicitly non-partisan.

Rule 17: No one should be compelled to vote by force or fines. Even though a number of democracies compel participation, this practice reflects little more than the naive view that high turnout is 'good' and low turnout is 'bad'. People choose to vote or to abstain for a great many reasons, but compelling them to do so does not make an election fair or competitive. It merely gives the state another excuse to interfere in our personal lives, and another way for it to tax.

Rule 18: Elections should not be judged invalid merely because turnout falls below some arbitrary threshold. If few citizens wish to participate, it is their free choice to allow the final outcome to be determined by those who do. Establishing a minimum turnout requirement merely gives citizens the opportunity to protest without incurring even the minimal cost of walking to the voting booth.

Rule 19: Elections should be regularly scheduled and not thrust suddenly upon an electorate. Too often this rule is violated to give incumbents special advantage. Sometimes that strategy is effective and sometimes it is not (a classic failure is Yeltsin's attempt to manipulate events by calling for new parliamentary elections before the rubble from the old parliament had been cleared away – rubble that hardly interfered with Zhirinovsky's campaign), but in either case, the election cannot be deemed fair.

Ensuring that all of these requirements are satisfied can be difficult. In Russia today, for example, there are suspicions of widespread vote fraud, since the administration of elections belongs largely to those whose fates depend on the outcome of those elections. We can only hope that, as representation becomes more meaningful and important to citizens, citizens themselves will demand electoral reform to guard against fraud. However, rather than lament that some of our criteria may be difficult to satisfy, it is more useful to consider something that does not appear on our list; namely the requirement that all candidates share equal resources (money) in a campaign. This supposition arises naturally out of the fear that unrestricted democratic process gives too great an advantage to the rich, to monied interests within society or to those who are willing to sell themselves to those interests. These concerns arise especially in societies that are experiencing primitive forms of capitalism in their transition to a market economy, owing to the perception (and to the fact) of extensive corruption in government. There is the temptation to restrict the ability of candidates and parties to raise money, and there is the parallel temptation to require the public financing of campaigns so as to equalize matters.

This argument has merit, and these concerns exist in established democracies if only because they have developed well-defined channels whereby money can flow from 'special interests' to politicians. However, against these concerns we must balance the idea that people participate in politics in many ways. They contribute not only money, but also time, energy and ideas. Do these contributions, and people's different abilities to make them, also violate any principle of fairness? And if we try to equalize resources across candidates, do we do this for all candidates and parties – including crazy extremists or those who can secure only their own vote?

Clearly, any idea can be carried to extremes. We cannot eliminate the influence of money or wholly equalize its availability. But there is in any argument for public financing of campaigns an implicit assumption that, unless uncovered, allows a naive view of politics. That assumption is that money operates in only one direction – to the disadvantage of those who do not have it. We are reminded here of the words of James Madison, the principal architect of the American constitution: 'The most common and durable source of [political] faction has been the various and unequal distribution of property'. From this excerpt we might infer that Madison foresaw the same class struggle as did Marx. To the contrary, however, he went on to note that, 'a landed interest, a manufacturing interest, a mercantile interest, a monied interest, with many lesser interests, grow up of necessity in civilized nations, and divide them into different classes, actuated by different sentiments and views'. Thus rather than view money as operating in any simple way so as to divide society into separate and permanent classes, Madison foresaw that the clash of interests would be multi-faceted and would divide society in innumerable ways.

For the most part, this has in fact been the course of history in stable democracies. Workers, businessmen, bankers or the 'middle class' rarely, if ever, vote with anything approaching unanimity. The trade policies of one party aid some sectors of the economy and workers in them, but damage and are opposed by others. The state subsidies that a candidate advocates may aid one industry, but only at the expense of those other parts of society that must pay for those subsidies. Farm policy assists one part of the agricultural sector, but often does so at the expense of another sector. An administration's decision to regulate prices and entry in one sector of an economy so as to bar competition injures those other sectors that use the output of the first as their input.

Politics in a stable democracy, then, is not dominated by the clash of class interests. There are too many interests for any category to predominate over the rest, and most interests cut across society in so many ways that they make that society look less like a layer cake and more like scrambled eggs. Workers hold investments in firms directly or through pension funds and thus are concerned about stock prices. Bankers are as concerned as anyone else with the cost of financing a new home or automobile – few are presidents riding in limousines. Trade policies that hurt one industry and aid another encourage alliances that cut across divisions of management and labour. And regional interests bisect almost any interest that does not correlate with geography. Moreover, if a policy aids one clearly definable segment of society at the expense of the rest, then generally that segment is too small to sustain itself as a winning coalition. And in the event that this segment is large – pensioners, veterans or farmers – there are other issues that divide these segments into opposing interests.

Parties and candidates must try to form winning coalitions in this scramble of interests, and it is here that we find an important source of democratic stability. We begin with the fact that the complexity of modern society makes any coalition of voters or legislators inherently vulnerable to disruption. Regardless of what combination of interests a politician might use to craft a winning coalition, the opposition can chip away at this support by offering some new advantage to elements of that coalition by framing an issue that divides it. This 'chipping away', however, occurs in all directions and along all dimensions – no coalition is invulnerable to disruption from any direction. The inherent instability of winning coalitions, in turn, makes all interests potentially pivotal. Indeed once a winning coalition is formed, all of its components can claim to be as critical to its existence as any other, thereby giving all a claim to the fruits of victory.

This coalitional instability need not translate into regime instability. It can strengthen it. Winners today, uncertain that they will not become losers tomorrow, are confronted with two choices. First, once in control they can try to maintain power by undemocratic means. This choice is viable, however, only if a significant part of society allows such actions. The second choice is to treat one's adversaries as they would wish their adversaries to treat them. Indeed the inherent instability of coalitions tells everyone that even if one loses power, there is a reasonable chance of regaining it in the future. And to the extent that the prospect of regaining power moderates the actions of those out of power, it also moderates the actions of those in power. All victories and all defeats are temporary.

Coalitional instability facilitates political stability in another way. If society consists of a complex array of cross-cutting interests, then the salience of issues that are especially disruptive of stability – ethnic and racial matters – diminishes. If different ethnic, linguistic or racial groups share economic and social concerns, coalitions based on emotional appeals to these dangerous cleavages can, in principle, be disrupted, and voters who are on different sides of some ethnic cleavage can be courted by the same candidates and parties who will have an incentive to moderate the salience of ethnic issues.

Of course, nothing we have said applies if elections are not fair and competitive. Voters must be able to implement the threat of punishing those who violate the norms of democratic process. And politicians must allow themselves to become temporary losers in the hope of becoming winners in the future. For a state accustomed to authoritarian rule in which winners vanquished losers, all of these things require a restructuring of beliefs about the consequences of winning and losing. Winners must come to believe that they will be punished at the polls for acting undemocratically, and losers must believe that, by playing the game of democratic politics skilfully, they can become winners. This restructuring is generally difficult, because beliefs change slowly and only with experience. Thus it is often said that the most critical election in a new democracy is the second, or at least the second in which there is a transfer of power. Once this election occurs, society's self-confidence in its democratic institutions is increased to the point where these new beliefs begin to predominate over the old ones. The trick, then, is to 'hold on' through the first few elections, since thereafter, if all other institutions are appropriately designed, fair and competitive elections will become a self-enforcing reality.

6. Economics or Politics: Which is the Chicken and Which the Egg?

Freed from authoritarian rule and the heavy hand of state control, the government of some newly formed democracy proceeds on the path of economic reform, basking in the glow of successful revolution and enthusiasm over new-found political freedom. But change soon generates undesirable side effects – unemployment, inflation, disparities in the distribution of wealth, corruption, illegality and violence. Enthusiasm is replaced by dissatisfaction and impatience, especially when the anticipated foreign aid and investment fail to materialize. Seeking to dampen discontent, the government makes bold promises it cannot keep or increases subsidies to failing industries. But dissatisfaction grows and champions of alternative policies multiply. Fearing a loss of power, the government vacillates between new decrees (some undemocratic) and accommodation with its critics. In the first instance, reform is clear and decisive (though not necessarily correct); in the second it is blurred by confusion and indecision. But vacillation between dictatorial decrees and soothing compromise, between policies formed by technocrats and policies formed by political holdovers from an earlier regime, and between rapid reform and no reform at all, erodes the government's ability to generate public support for any new decisive economic action. Soon only criminals or entrenched bureaucrats have control, and democracy becomes a sham since neither criminals nor bureaucrats seem willing to allow voters to dictate their role. Frustrated with the incapacity of democrats, with the disintegration of the state and with the threat to national sovereignty implicit in a state ruled by drug lords and pimps, the military acts!

Although this scenario, or at least its early stages, can describe any of the successor states of the Soviet Union, it also describes any number of countries in Eastern Europe and Latin America that have attempted political and economic reform simultaneously. As a consequence, no small number of countries have seen their transition to democracy derailed by a military dictatorship or a 'palace coup' that seizes power with the argument that only it can stabilize events and pull the country out of chaos.

An especially salient question, then, is whether it is better to implement democratic reforms as quickly as possible along with market reforms, or whether we should postpone political reform so the move to a market economy can be directed by decisive action. Which comes first: political or economic change? Can a transition to democracy facilitate a prosperous economy or is a prosperous economy a necessary condition for stable democracy? Is democracy possible when inflation exceeds 1000 per cent and prices are quoted in foreign currencies that only some élite can earn? Should a new constitution be adopted after the economy is reformed or should it be considered along with economic changes?

These questions do not arise merely because political turmoil appears only to exacerbate economic difficulties. They arise also because at almost the same time as the Soviet Union and Eastern Europe began their political liberalization, China embarked on its economic reforms but rejected political ones. Today, even though we must appreciate that it began at a pitifully low starting point, we see China as a whole experiencing one of the highest economic growth rates in the world. The Soviet Union has passed into history, with each of its former republics subject to double-digit rates of economic decline. These questions arise also because opponents of political liberalization point to the economic 'miracles' of South Korea, Chile, Taiwan and Japan, all of which had their economies directed by an oligarchy that did not confront competitive elections until recently, if at all. Each of these countries (and there are others) illustrates successful economic development without recourse to the incoherence of the Soviet Union's erstwhile democratic politics.

In one sense, then, the answer to all of our questions about the direction and order of reform is simple: if economic reform is to proceed along a well-defined path, then it is not unreasonable to postpone the transition to democracy in favour of the enlightened despot who does 'democratic things' when such things are required and who transgresses on democratic rights only when there is no alternative.

Unfortunately, this answer poses practical difficulties. First, what if there is no consensus about reform? What if some want to proceed slowly and others quickly? What if some want to privatize everything – industries, collective farms and retail stores – while others want only to privatize particular things? What if some want to protect against the threat of massive unemployment while others are more concerned about the prospect of hyperinflation? And what if some see the necessity for deep sacrifice among urban and rural poor while others are willing to trade such sacrifice for a less severe but more uncertain package of economic reforms?

Second, what guarantee do we have that the postponement of political reform favours the selection of an enlightened despot who will relinquish power and implement democracy at the appropriate time? China's leaders protected their despotism by killing and jailing opponents without regret; authorities are still looking for the victims of repression in Chile and Argentina; Taiwan's Kuomingtang Party jailed its political adversaries and, in its early history on the island, acted much like its communist counterpart on the mainland; news reporters continue to cover student riots in South Korea and ruling élites must live in the shadow of an unsavory past; and in Japan official corruption at the highest levels, despite the damage inflicted on governmental stability, seems a way of life. It should also be kept in mind, moreover, that these 'economic miracles' owe as much to the role of the United States in their economies as they do to any inspired leadership. Even today, China's growth could not be sustained without investment from, and trade with, Taiwan, Japan and the United States and from wage rates and labour practices that would repulse citizens in any stable democracy.

All we have said thus far, however, establishes that there are dangers along any path to reform. So let us look at the fundamental problem that confronts economic reform in an ex-communist state and begin from there. Briefly, that problem is the almost complete absence of property rights. Without 'property rights' – without the enforceable right of ownership and the corresponding right to buy, sell and trade, as well as other economic freedoms – markets uncorrupted by guns and violence cannot develop. With 'property rights' the state can abrogate at its discretion, and with contracts that are unenforceable in any court, efficient markets cannot exist. Without these things, economic reform remains but another version of state ownership, central planning or war-lordism, with all of the economic inefficiencies and threats to individual liberties that these things imply.

This is not to say that citizens of Russia, Ukraine, Belarus, Kazakhstan and elsewhere do not feel a sense of ownership. Apartments can be traded, goods and services can be bought in open (if inefficient) markets, and workers and management can capture some of the profits (if any) from their employment. But legal systems for defining, monitoring and protecting these rights are primitive. A system of property rights is something more than a set of labels that say 'I own this' or 'You own that'. It also includes political and legal institutions whereby people and firms can defend these labels against expropriation, whereby they can resolve disputes over labels, and whereby new rights can be defined as technology, opinion and circumstances change.

Without these rights and ways to assign them, and without ways to protect them once assigned, markets cannot develop, investments will not be made and new technologies will not arise. The transition to a market economy, then, is something more than the privatization of state property and the issuing of vouchers. This transition requires political institutional development: legislatures to create the laws that will define and protect rights as well as coherent tax codes; courts to interpret and enforce those laws; elections to direct the legislature and political parties to mobilize the population to political action and give their preferences a voice; and a government that feels sufficiently responsive to political pressures that it will act against at least the most corrupt and violent practices of whatever criminal element seeks to take advantage of the economic and political disequilibrium.

But now we come to the core question of economic and political transition: are there policies that democratic systems are inherently incapable of implementing but that are necessary for successful economic reform? Is a democracy capable of creating the system of property rights that a market economy requires, or must those rights and the institutions associated with their evolution and enforcement be set in place by an autocratic regime?

The problem, of course, is that reform is never smooth. Reform is necessarily accompanied by unpleasant things: unemployment, sagging investment, a decline in living standards for all but a select few, the erosion of savings through inflation, increased crime and the deterioration of social services. And, as in the scenario that introduces this chapter, these dislocations create political demands to stall or reverse reforms that governments, especially democratic ones, find difficult to resist. In contrast, the authoritarian state – one that controls the military or internal security police – seems better equipped to resist these pressures, to pursue reform with single-minded determination, to jail nearly anyone, and to try to substitute state power for market incentives whenever necessary. Thus although we may have to sacrifice on the issue of human rights, it seems reasonable to suppose that the authoritarian state is better positioned to implement the bitter medicine of reform.

But before we accept the superiority of authoritarian rule, let us consider more carefully the presumed failings of democracy. We want to argue that the fault is not with democracy *per se*, but with an incompletely formed democracy. If economic and political reform proceed simultaneously, then the democratic transition is incomplete by definition at the time economic reforms are begun. Constitutions are not yet drafted, or if drafted are poorly understood; their provisions have not yet been implemented by legislative action; and if implemented, the courts are only beginning to develop ways to enforce the law. Thus political leaders and public officials have at best only a weak relationship to the different interests in society, and these interests are often poorly organized and can exert political pressure in only the crudest ways.

The best organized interests in a newly formed democracy are those whose only common interest was their opposition to the old regime or those who believe that they can proceed with 'business as usual' under any regime. These interests are dominated by those with weak or non-existent preferences for successful reform: bureaucrats with little incentive to compromise on anything that requires fewer resources being committed to the public sector; managers of state-subsidized firms that prefer anything but competitive markets; and leaders of specialized unions that represent but a small percentage of the labour force. Thus of the two approaches that a government commonly takes in a newly formed democracy – accommodation and decrees – the second, after revealing the true costs of transition, exacerbates the problem of support by focusing all responsibility on a small subset of technocrats which lacks the power or will to force compliance to its actions. The first course, accommodation, cannot work simply because it seeks an alliance of contradictory forces.

The usual failure of simultaneous political and economic reform is not too much democracy but too little. With political institutions that do not yet accommodate the range of social interests, with property rights still undefined and the institutions for defining them ill-formed, and with electoral institutions that do not allow voters to sanction public officials so that they have a self-interest consonant with the interests of the rest of society, the policies that emerge from accommodation are equivalent to policy by decree, except that now no one holds responsibility for its failure. Although they may have the appearance of democratic compromise, these policies have not been formed in a democratic way. As the product of temporary alliances among élites with contradictory preferences, they have little long-term economic or political justification. They are not policies designed by leaders of political parties with long-term goals of re-election who need to develop a broad base of mass political support. If they are the correct policies, they are correct by accident. Those party to the accommodation do not confront the necessity of having to explain their decisions to anyone but other élites. Their arena of conflict is among themselves. Because they lack electoral responsibility, they lack democratic responsibility. Their primary objective is to position themselves for succession to power. The incompletely formed democracy, then, combines the worst of both worlds: authoritarian rule by a committee that answers only to itself.

But those who oppose a full move to democracy – a new constitution, regularly scheduled elections, a new legislature, new courts and new laws – will object that, 'the people are unprepared for democracy. They do not yet understand the give-and-take of such politics and they will be too easily led astray by demagogues'. Wouldn't a more concerted move to democracy during a period of economic turmoil merely result in a replay of Weimar Germany's experience?

Germany, though, illustrates our argument that incomplete democracy poses special dangers. Hitler's accession to power was not the result of simple mass unrest; rather it was also the product of a poorly designed political system that was incapable of accommodating social tensions and implementing coherent policy – a system that virtually guaranteed governmental instability and a confusion of roles between president and parliament. Hitler was selected as chancellor by precisely those élites who would have objected most strongly to complete democratic freedom.

In fact warnings of the unavoidable dangers of democracy are too often uttered by those who know little about it. Why should we suppose that *apparatchiks* and members of the nomenclatura can judge what is required for democratic process? How do they know that the 'masses' are too ignorant to act in their own self-interest? Where is it proved that acting democratically is more difficult than running a tractor or maintaining a household? Are we better prepared beforehand to raise children than to vote? Why are those 'ignorant and easily misled masses' who emigrate to democracies from countries with little or no democratic tradition able to grasp quickly the essentials of organizing in their self-interest – is there something in the waters of Israel, the United States, Canada or Australia that makes immigrants suddenly wiser?

The assertion of ignorance and lack of preparation, we should remind ourselves, too often serves the self-interest of those who make these arguments. It is perhaps better to ask: what preparations are being made to inform people about democracy? What institutions of self-rule at the local and regional levels are being provided to 'train' voters and new political élites?

Nothing we have said implies that democratic transition in periods of economic turmoil does not pose great risks. Too many democracies have been launched with disastrous consequences for us to argue that we can proceed with unrestrained optimism. But there are also great risks associated with abiding by the assumption that there is a self-evident correct economic policy and that an autocrat will know and choose that policy. Finally, none of the presumed dangers of democracy mean that we cannot begin the process of democratic transition at the local level without any threat to the security of the state. It is here that people can practise and learn the mechanics of democracy. Democratic transition need not be 'top-down'. Just as the framers of the US constitution practised democracy first at the state and local levels in the 18th century, the citizens of Taiwan did the same in their transition to democracy in the 20th. Rather than a wholesale rejection of democratic reform in favour of authoritarianism, this is the lesson transitions to democracy teach. De Tocqueville's observation (*Democracy in America*) about America in the 1830s, then, that, 'the constitution of the United States is an admirable work, nevertheless one may believe that its founders would not have succeeded, had not the previous 150 years given the different states of the Union a taste for, and practice of, provincial governments' holds true for any state.

Finally, if we return once again to the issue of property rights, we should remind the reader that, before the break-up of the Soviet Union, the world's largest experiment in privatization did not occur in Britain, France or China. It occurred in the United States in the 19th century, when the federal government 'owned' virtually all land west of the Mississippi river (and a good share of the land east of it as well). In less than 100 years most of the usable parts of that land were privatized so that, even with the 'distraction' of a civil war, America began the 20th century as the world's largest and most productive economy. Certainly corruption and avarice characterized the process of privatization and not a few great fortunes were made with means of questionable legality. But the chief mechanism whereby the land was turned to productive use was simple and straightforward: property rights secured by democratic institutions. Economic prosperity did not bring democracy to America's west; democracy came first, and was subsequently refined as prosperity appeared.

7. Constitutional Rights: Mere Words or Sustainable Guarantees?

Citizens and political élites in most countries moving from the shadows of communism are schizophrenic. On the one hand, they are sceptical about democracy as a route to a prosperous future, and they are suspicious of the value of a constitution as a meaningful guarantor of individual rights and civil liberties. On the other hand, those who would write constitutions for these countries offer drafts replete with promises, directives and rights in a form that suggests that they believe every word will be faithfully executed.

Finding the source of this schizophrenia requires that we move to first principles – to the ways in which individual rights are secured in a democracy. We begin by noting that establishing any state requires granting its various parts the right to coordinate us, through coercion if necessary, so we can accomplish things that will not be accomplished otherwise. Thus acting as our agent, we allow the state to tax and to spend, to draft, to legislate and, in the event of illegality, to imprison. In ages past this coercive and coordinative function was claimed and imposed by a small élite. Today democracies are constituted with the understanding that the state should serve only with the consent of the governed and that the governed hold the ultimate voice in how the state acts. The great trick of democratic design, however, lies in constructing the state so that public officials do not exceed their authority.

An important part of this 'trick' is an appropriately designed constitution, which, in addition to defining the components of the state and their relationship to each other and to the people, sets limits on the state's power. But in drafting such a document two questions arise:

1. How can a piece of paper control anything, let alone those who direct the state's coercive parts and who might aspire to despotism or whose ego might lead them to believe that only they know what is best?
2. What is it that properly belongs in such a document – what should

be made specific, what should be made ambiguous and what issues should it confront?

These two questions converge when drafting constitutional guarantees of fundamental rights – those individual rights that define a free and just society. Some of these rights are well-understood and appear in virtually every democratic constitution, such as a guarantee of religious freedom, of the freedom of the press, of the right to peaceful assembly, of the inviolability of personal property, of equality in the right to vote, and of the right to a speedy and fair trial. The inclusion of other 'rights' – welfare entitlements – is more controversial, such as a guarantee of housing, employment and just compensation for labour. Our two questions, then, combine to form a third, namely: why should the second category of 'rights' be controversial, but not those in the first category?

Before we address these questions, there is a related matter that requires attention: the advisability of including citizen obligations or duties in a constitution. Put simply, clauses requiring, for example, that, 'man's exercise of his rights and liberties must not…be detrimental to the public weal or surrounding environment', that, 'everyone…display concern for the preservation of the historical and cultural heritage', that, 'everyone …pay taxes…in the amounts established by law' or that, 'parents have the obligation to raise and support their children' – are dangerous not merely because they can serve no useful democratic purpose, but also because they pervert the function of the constitution. First:

Rule 20: Lists of citizen obligations in a constitution pervert a constitution's bill of rights by diffusing its primary intent: keeping states from tyranny. A constitution defines and places limits on the state and not on the sovereign, the people.

Rule 21: Such clauses serve no useful purpose. If people choose to place limits on themselves, they can do so through their representative assemblies, via the laws they allow those assemblies to pass.

Rule 22: Lists of citizen obligations are dangerous. They establish the precedent that a constitution can control and limit rights rather than protect them.

We can attribute such clauses to the fear of ambiguity, especially when it appears that the full expression of a person's rights might conflict with someone else's, and to the fear that people will not know their responsibilities as citizens. But here it is best to rely on a legislative or judicial resolution, as well as on the ability of people to learn their roles and responsibilities. If the other parts of our constitution are designed well, we can rely on the structure a constitution establishes to reach a just accommodation whenever rights appear to conflict and to guide our learning; if they are designed poorly, it matters little what rights and duties we specify.

Turning to the issue of what rights belong in a constitution, we should note that the state's role with respect to 'aspirations' can be decided as part of normal politics, but only if other rights are secure. If citizens are free to engage in political discourse, informed by a viable press, and able to displace one set of leaders with another, then they can use the state, if they so choose, to secure fair compensation for labour, safe working conditions, adequate housing, environmental protection and pensions. But if they lose basic rights, attainment or retention of these things is at best problematical and at worst subject to the whim of an otherwise tyrannical state. Indeed a society unable to partake of its fundamental rights has no protection against the avaricious official who acts in his narrow self-interest, regardless of the aspirations otherwise provided for in a constitution. Tradition may dictate the inclusion of aspirations in a constitution. But such things should not be confused with basic rights. We can direct the state to be concerned with just compensation for labour and health care. But requiring that the state *ensure* just compensation or that it *guarantee* medical care opens the door to contentious judicial and political processes as people attempt to decide whether legislation moves us close enough to the required goal. Should we declare a medical care bill unconstitutional because it only takes us part way to a wholly comprehensive solution to public health or would we prefer to view such legislation as an essential first step? More problematical is the fact that the state may be unable to satisfy such requirements, in which case its failure to satisfy these 'rights' undermines confidence that it will act to ensure others. Thus:

> *Rule 23*: Constitutions should make aspirations irrelevant to a court's deliberations so that they can focus on whether legislation is in conformity with fundamental constitutional rights.

Turning to fundamental rights, the safest way to approach matters is with a healthy dose of cynicism about how public officials will interpret various provisions. The prudent assumption is that legislators, bureaucrats and the like will operate in their own self-interest and that even a viable electoral system can only imperfectly regulate this self-interest. Thus although the other parts of the constitution should ensure that these motives are the correct ones, history has taught us the value of additional precautions. Among these precautions is a succinct statement of each right:

> *Rule 24*: Long or convoluted clauses detailing individual rights cannot substitute for simple admonitions and unqualified restrictions on state action.

Compare, for example, the American provision that the legislature, 'shall pass no law abridging the freedom of the press' with the more ambiguously identified 'right' in an early Russian draft constitution that, 'the media are free…[but] the seizure and confiscation of information material and the hardware for its preparation and transmission are permitted only in accordance with a ruling by a court of law'. Although such qualification may be designed to ensure flexibility in the event of unforeseen contingencies, it opens the door to judicial confusion as to original intent, and gives the bureaucrat and politician room to circumvent that intent. Concise statements of rights provide the court, moreover, with a valuable weapon in their defence of rights and in their inevitable conflicts with executive and legislative branches. Society may choose to adhere to certain qualifications (like a prohibition against shouting 'fire' in a theatre). But as with those instances in which rights might conflict, the way in which qualifications are best arrived at is a social consensus reached through legitimate political process rather than through constitutional edict. If consensual – if such qualifications assume the role of a social norm about civil conduct – then they can be easily specified and enforced through normal legislation.

But before we can write a concise constitutional delineation of rights, we must answer the question: what rights are an essential part of any democratic constitution? What is the common characteristic of those rights we normally think of as 'basic': the right to free speech, to assemble peacefully, to a speedy and fair trial, to protection of our property, to the free choice of religious conviction, and so on? The answer to these questions is contained in the core characteristic of democracy: that the people, and only the people, are sovereign and that the state is merely the sovereign's agent. Thus:

Rule 25: A right is basic and essential if its abrogation undermines the authority of the sovereign to control the sovereign's agent, the state. And since control in a democracy is exercised primarily through elections, a right is basic and essential if its abrogation undermines our ability to displace one set of leaders with another through election.

We protect speech, then, because it is impossible to have free and fair elections without the ability to confront political leaders with accusations of incompetence or even criminality; we allow adjustments in this right (again, as with prohibitions against yelling 'fire' in a crowded theatre) because it does not limit our ability to control the state. We protect the right of free and peaceful assembly, since free and fair elections are impossible if the sovereign cannot organize opposition to the state outside of the state's formal structure. We protect the right to petition the state for redress of grievances, since the sovereign should be allowed to convey its wants to those who hold official position so that they can adjust their policies accordingly. We protect religious freedom since, if the state can control our religious institutions, it can control all manner of thought and thereby undermine the essence of free democratic choice. We guarantee due process of law since we cannot have free and fair elections if the state can use its judicial arm to coerce or jail opponents. We ensure against discrimination on the basis of race, religion, sex and ethnicity since we cannot allow the state to use the principle of majority rule to abrogate the ability of minorities to participate fully in democratic process. And we protect the right to property not merely to have efficient markets but also to preclude the state from coercing us with threats of expropriation and government-sanctioned theft.

We arrive finally at the most fundamental question, the one that forms the title to this chapter: how are these basic and essential rights enforced? Certainly we should not suppose that merely setting words to paper provides any iron-clad guarantee. Too much history tells us otherwise. Instead the answer lies in the incentives of public officials that other parts of the constitution establish.

Constitutions seek to do more than merely define the various branches of the state with the idea that a bill of rights will protect us against any usurpation of power by these branches. The institutions a constitution establishes control the aspirations of officials by 'setting ambition against ambition' (Madison, *Federalist Papers*). This is accomplished in three ways:

1. It creates a balance of power among the separate branches of government. In presidential systems, executive, legislative and judicial branches are explicitly separate. In parliamentary systems, the executive is fused with the legislative, but the executive (prime minister) is given the authority (in conjunction, perhaps, with a president or monarch) to dissolve the legislature and call for new elections.
2. It gives the different branches of the government a different relation to the people. Thus a president is elected directly by all citizens; legislators are elected by smaller constituencies; and the court is selected indirectly by the people through joint legislative–executive action. In this way political leaders confront each other with as great a variety of interests as possible, so that public policy must be passed with some minimal level of consensus.
3. In large or heterogeneous states such as Russia, the United States and Switzerland, a federal governmental structure allows citizens to control as much of their destiny as possible in a part of government closest to them, and ensures that local and regional concerns are given full weight at the national governmental level.

All of this structure influences the incentives of political leaders to protect rights. If the system is designed correctly – if political careers depend on protecting rights or ensuring against bureaucratic infringement of rights – then those rights are preserved. Otherwise those rights are mere words on paper. Individual rights frequently succumbed to political ambition in Latin America not because the lists of rights in the constitutions were incomplete, but because the political systems did not function to them. And they were sometimes ignored in the United States, especially on racial matters, not because they failed to be well articulated, but rather because there was no consensual will to pay full heed to them and, correspondingly, because politicians gained little political capital by acting otherwise.

What is evident from this abbreviated answer to our question, then, is that the mechanism whereby rights are protected and the public interest served depends on a complex interaction of all parts of the government, in combination with the people's consensual determination to keep those rights. Thus when evaluating some part of a constitution, we must calculate how that part fits into the larger scheme of things. A debate over the appropriate relationship of the executive to the legislature cannot be resolved without also considering, among other things, the federal construction of the state, the likely character of political parties and the relationship of each branch of government to voters Similarly, in ascertaining whether a constitution grants local or regional government sufficient autonomy requires that we evaluate the extent to which the parts of the national government have an incentive to maintain that autonomy. This depends on whether national politicians will be led to care sufficiently about local interests, which in turn depends on whether people prefer to defend regional interests and regional governmental prerogatives against incursions by the national government. Completing the circle, this in turn depends on whether the state as a whole is structured so as to encourage that interest among its citizens.

8. Democratic Institutions: Why Would They Influence Anything?

This volume's theme is that the design of democratic institutions – constitutions, electoral laws, forms of legislative representation, and so on – can greatly influence outcomes, including the stability of the state itself. But why should we believe that institutions will influence anything? Don't fundamental forces, historical inevitabilities and the intervention of powerful personalities determine the flow of events? Isn't it more important to ensure that society chooses the correct leaders? Why should we suppose that 'democratic' institutions will not merely provide legal cover for the few who act to the detriment of the many? And how can institutions that seem alien to a society's traditions and alien to the social theories that justified an earlier regime change politics meaningfully?

These are profoundly important questions because they take us to the source of democratic stability and to the basis for asserting that democracy is a preferred form of social organization. Thus they warrant answers before we proceed further in this series to discussions of alternative institutional forms. We begin, then, with the fact that every society operates by rules that define admissible and inadmissible, encouraged and discouraged, behaviour. In primitive societies, these rules often appear as tradition and religious prescription. More modern societies set some of their rules to paper as laws, but most rules remain implicit and are referred to as 'social norms'. A norm may be a simple thing such as allowing those on a bus to exit before those who wish to enter move; or it may be more complex, as when it prescribes whom to give one's seat to on a bus and when to do so. Simple or complex, these norms guide behaviour on a day-to-day basis and it is difficult to imagine society without them.

But why do people allow themselves to be bound by norms, especially if, as is often the case, there are no laws to ensure compliance? The short answer is that society, implicitly aware of the order they provide and the benefits that flow from order, achieves a consensus about acceptable patterns of behaviour and teaches them to successive generations so that they become 'automatic'. At the same time, society sanctions those who defect from its norms, and so it must also establish norms that govern the application of these sanctions. Shoving one's way on to a bus before all who wish to leave it have done so may ensure a seat, but most persons avoid such behaviour because they know what everyone thinks of such acts – and few persons want to be scolded publicly by someone's grandmother. Norms of conduct on public transportation are adhered to, then, because it is not in a person's self-interest to act otherwise. And the norm is enforced because those who enforce – the grandmother who scolds – know that their actions are effective and acceptable.

Social norms cease serving their purpose when people believe that others will not adhere to them, when people fail to impose the requisite sanctions, or when they become confused over which norms are legitimate and which are illegitimate. Society, then, can encounter 'a crisis of norms' when it tries to establish new social and economic relations. If we are told in one month that private profit is a crime and in the next that it is a social virtue or that the accumulation of private property has been transformed from an act of exploitation to a right, then it may take some time before a new system of norms emerges to render society coherent and efficient.

Most norms come to us 'automatically' and, unsure of their source, we relegate their study to sociology and anthropology. But the 'norms of democracy' are established differently. These norms, which include such things as honouring individual rights provided for in a constitution, arise at least initially through acts of conscious creation. In fact the most explicit and expansive act of norm-creation is drafting a political constitution that specifies the restrictions that define the legitimate actions of the state.

In times past the norms of legitimate political action were directed at citizens and enforced by monarchs or dictators. There was no confusion over their content and little reason for most of us to become concerned with their genesis. Our primary concern was to make certain that we did not violate them. In turn, the security of the ultimate enforcer of these norms – the monarch or dictator himself – derived from our common fear and belief that if any person or small group acted otherwise, sanctions would be applied. No matter how well or poorly the dictator or monarch governed, we knew the cost of deviation, including the cost of failing to participate in a sanction we believed unjust. Revolutions, then, occur when a large enough part of society comes to believe that they will not be punished or, out of ideological or patriotic conviction, that the benefits of defection exceed the likely personal costs.

The transition to democracy is also a conscious process, except that unlike when a dictator asserts his will, democratic transition entails the establishment of a set of norms that are based on the principles of self-governance, the rule of law and respect for individual rights. A constitution, in turn, is the central component of this norm-generating process because it defines the institutions of governance – courts, legislatures, electoral laws and executive offices – and it defines the relation of these institutions to each other and to the people. These institutions are like norms because they consist of bundles of rules. The description of a legislature, for example, includes the rules whereby its members are elected, the rules that define legitimate and illegitimate political opposition, the rules under which voters vote and political parties operate to fill legislative seats, the rules that dictate legislative deliberations, and the rules that specify how the products of those deliberations (laws) are to be ultimately enforced.

That the construction of a democratic society focuses on the creation of institutions is one of the things that distinguishes it from an earlier, failed experiment. That experiment, the communist one, was predicated on the assumption that fundamental values would change and that people would come to equate private and social values. The assumption was that people could be 'perfected' to pursue purely social values. Those who could not be 'perfected' were simply eliminated, and little attention was given to guiding self-interest through the creation of new institutional structures. Although the leadership of the party or the dictate of an autocrat would substitute during any transitional period, eventually the state would 'wither away' so temporary repression could substitute for institutional design. That idea is now bankrupt: values and beliefs cannot be divorced from individual self-interest and, as we have learned all too painfully, the autocrat can too easily pervert the institutions he controls.

Democracy operates with a different assumption: to reiterate James Madison's famous premise, 'the seeds of faction are sown in the nature of man'. Hence rather than try to perfect people, democracy seeks instead to redirect self-interest and to develop a consensus about norms of an entirely different type. It seeks to develop norms about the legitimacy of procedures, rules and institutional structures that channel self-interest in socially acceptable ways and in ways that re-enforce people's incentives to maintain those institutions. Thus when we speak of a country as having a democratic tradition or democratic consciousness, we do not mean that its citizens are somehow more perfect or pursue different ends than people elsewhere. We mean that they share a consensus over the legitimacy of particular institutions and individual rights, that they expect their fellow citizens to act in accordance with the rules that describe those institutions, that they have incentives to sanction those who act contrary to these expectations, and that those who do act contrary to these expectations in fact expect to be sanctioned.

If the act of democratic norm-creation is performed well, these norms direct people's actions as intended; if designed poorly, they either fail to influence actions or they influence them in unintended and undesirable ways. But now we come to the critical question: what determines whether these norms, these bundles of rules, are designed well or poorly? How do we know that a constitution is complete or incomplete, well or poorly crafted, appropriate for a society or inappropriate?

Our other chapters try to give substance to different parts of the answers to these questions by focusing on specific institutions and processes. But in providing details, we should not lose sight of the mechanism whereby constitutional rules are enforced. Democratic institutions and rules that work well are followed and enforced in much the same way as are social norms. The politician who contemplates an action that dishonours his position, the legislator who subverts parliamentary procedure and potential tyrants will be constrained from these actions if they believe that existing political institutions give society the incentive to sanction such actions, if those institutions coordinate society to resist this subversion so that their self-interest is to act otherwise. The great trick to constructing stable democratic institutions, then, is this: rules (or the bundles of rules we call institutions) that are consistent with the normative values we associate with democratic practice – the values specified in a bill of rights – must be constructed so that it is in everyone's interest to abide by them, so that it is in society's interest to punish defectors (as when voters act to defeat an incumbent politician), so that we do not create incentives for subsequent detrimental changes in institutional structure, and so that the outcomes that eventually emerge are deemed as beneficial as those that any other feasible configuration of institutions can generate. Satisfying this requirement imposes at least the following general restrictions on feasible institutions and workable rules:

Rule 26: Democratic rules must be unambiguous. A rule such as 'the legislature will pass no law infringing on the freedom of the press' may seem in want of qualification (to avoid, say, the publication of pornography). But if there is a consensus over acceptable qualifications and if society's other political institutions are well crafted (if, for example, the legislature that appoints judges is responsive to society), the exceptions the courts allow will be acceptable. Similarly, we cannot leave electoral procedures ambiguous, lest those who fill public office manipulate those procedures to their own advantage.

Rule 27: Rules must be consistent. The rules of democratic process contradict each other, as when, for example, we give both a legislature and a president the constitutional authority to promulgate laws or when we give two government agencies jurisdiction over the same policy. Constitutions, then, should be examined as an exercise in logic, just as a mathematician checks the proof of a new theorem – by examining the proof for completeness and logical consistency.

Rule 28: Democratic institutions and rules should be promulgated under the assumption that public office holders will try to subvert those rules and procedures whenever it is in their interest to do so. Internal checks on the abuse of power – a presidential veto, judicial review of legislation, legislative oversight of the courts – are an essential component of democratic rules.

Rule 29: Democratic rules, especially constitutional ones, need to 'fit together' lest the law of unintended consequences operate with special force. Constitutions, then, cannot be written merely by taking different parts of the constitutional documents of other states as a child might choose candy in a candy store – 'I'll take one of those, one of those', and so on.

To this list we need to add one more item, namely that democratic rules must be manifestly fair. Rules cannot confer permanent advantage on one identifiable group at the expense of some other group. This is an especially difficult requirement to satisfy, since we do not mean by it that we merely give everyone an explicit guarantee of some minimal share of the spoils of politics. By themselves, such words are worthless guarantees. Instead we must constitute our rules and institutions so that the losers in any dispute can reasonably believe that they have a chance to become winners and that they are relevant to the resolution of future disputes. The particular difficulty here, however, is that although we can contribute to manifest fairness by the proper design of institutions, beliefs themselves are self-fulfilling prophecies. If people believe that the system is manifestly fair, then it will be; but if they believe otherwise, then it will be otherwise. If people believe that losing confers permanent disadvantage, they will act as if each battle is war. And if winners believe the same, then they must ensure that their victory is complete by vanquishing their opponents lest their opponents subsequently vanquish them. Thus how we satisfy the preceding requirements while at the same time constituting our rules so that they engender the correct beliefs is one of the things we address in the remaining chapters of this essay.

9.   A New Constitution: Should We Cut Trees to Print It?

Most states – democratic or otherwise – possess constitutions, but it is generally assumed that the transition to democracy requires new political institutions, new political traditions and thus a new constitution. However, the people in such societies can reasonably ask why they should expect anything better from a new document than from their old one. After all, Soviet constitutions promised freedom of speech, of assembly, the right to vote, a free press, the right to express one's grievances, guaranteed pensions, health care, housing, vacations, and so on...and look what happened there! What can possibly be written on paper that will change anything? Why should we regard the promises contained in a new piece of paper as anything more than part of a fraud perpetrated on society by a handful of political élites concerned primarily with maintaining their position? Wouldn't it be better and less deceitful to dispense with experiments in democracy, return to political structures more in keeping with tradition (monarchy, autocracy, dictatorship?), and get the economy functioning so that people needn't be hungry and cold?

Regardless of whether such questions are framed seriously or cynically, they require answers. Otherwise there is no reason to suppose that anyone will pay much attention to any new constitutional document, however well crafted it might be or however noble the intentions of its authors. And in that event, the prediction that the constitution is meaningless can only become a self-fulfilling prophecy.

What we want to argue here, however, is that the Soviet bloc experience with 'constitutionalism' should not result in pessimism or cynicism. Specifically, we want to explore the argument that that experience should either be deemed as merely irrelevant to any debate over a constitution's role in facilitating the transformation to democracy or that it should be interpreted to give us confidence that democratic constitutionalism will in fact work in ex-communist states. We realize, of course, that in offering the hypothesis that the past is as much a source of confidence as it is of pessimism, readers might believe that we have smoked or drunk too much of some foreign substance. Nevertheless, let us consider for the moment the Soviet Union's '77 constitution, adopted with great fanfare throughout the USSR in a process in which innumerable people wrote letters offering input to which political élites pretended to pay some heed.

The fault of that document was not that it somehow failed, but rather that it worked precisely as designed. Those who believe it failed owing to the gap between promise and reality are correct to assert that merely setting words to paper about rights and social welfare entitlements did not, and in general cannot, accomplish much. But this presumption of failure is based on a preoccupation with only one of three questions we can ask about a constitution when evaluating its performance. In this instance the question being asked is: did the constitution lead to the realization of stated individual rights and social guarantees? The answer, evident to everyone but the most diehard apologist of an old regime, is no, and therein lies the source of pessimism about the prospects for a democratic society guided by constitutional principles in the successor states of the Soviet Union today.

That question, however, is not the only one with which to evaluate the prospects for democracy, because it focuses on but one of the things we want from a constitution. Before we can reach any conclusions, we must also answer two additional questions: did the constitution legitimize or contribute to the stability of the political institutions it prescribed for society; and were those institutions appropriate for the realization of the rights and social guarantees identified as goals within the constitution? Only if our answers to these questions are no and yes can we deem a constitution a failure. In fact our answers are exactly the opposite.

The problem with Soviet constitutions was that they were based on a social theory that assumed that people are perfectible and that beliefs and values can be changed fundamentally so that social goals become private ones. Thus they enshrined a political system that could not realize those goals. However, although they failed to do what no constitution can do directly – guarantee the realization of lofty principles by mere proclamation – Soviet constitutions succeeded to the extent that the system and institutions they legitimized did in fact function as described. Setting Marxist–Leninist principles at the core of Soviet social organization, both the '36 and, even more forthrightly, the '77 constitutions did one thing: they legitimized the dictatorship of the

Communist Party. And having done that, all the rest became mere window-dressing.

This is not to say that those constitutions played a role in forming political structures: those structures existed before the writing of either document. But they did give legal sanction to what existed. Thus with respect to our second question about their influence on political structures, these facts should cause us to regard Soviet constitutions as either irrelevant to events or they should lead us to believe that they contributed to the strength of existing institutions. In either case, the answer to our second question ought to be yes.

Turning to our third question – the adequacy of that structure for realizing stated goals – the social theory on which Soviet constitutions were based failed to appreciate that a top-down command–control economy cannot function in a world where prosperity and security depend on a vibrant consumer economy, high technology and efficiently operating financial markets rather than on simple directives concerning the manufacture of steel, cement, tractors and tanks. More importantly, that theory also failed to anticipate the inevitable consequences of the unchecked political power of the Communist Party – inefficiency and corruption – which appear regardless of whether that power is entrusted to some committee or to an individual. Nevertheless, this was the structure that Soviet constitutions sought to legitimize, and this was the one that prevailed. And herein lies the reason why those constitutions failed to deliver on their promises: they legitimized a political system that may have tried initially to fulfil its promises, but they succumbed eventually to the fact that they did not legitimize institutions that would ensure that the pursuit of self-interest would serve the public interest. Thus, the answer to our third question is no.

So if there is a lesson to be learned from the USSR's constitutional experience, it is not that constitutions cannot work. Rather the lesson is either that the experience is an irrelevant experiment or that even bad constitutions can, for a time at least, be stable. Of course, this argument does not challenge the view that history would have been unchanged if any of these constitutions was a wholly democratic document or even a blank piece of paper. It need not convince anyone that a new constitution can lead to something other than what exists. It does not contradict the assertion that the Soviet Union or any of its successor states must proceed along historical paths that can only be interrupted but not negated by attempts at developing a constitutional democracy. To counter these arguments requires consideration of the more general matter of how constitutions in fact influence political processes, how they ensure rights and how they facilitate the establishment of stable political systems.

We cannot address all of these issues here, but we can indicate how to avoid the excesses that occurred previously. Briefly, the core of any constitution, aside from rights, is a specification of a governmental structure that defines the relations of its different parts (the executive, legislature and judiciary) to each other and to the sovereign, the people. Their varied relations to the people determine the extent to which each part will find it in its interest to reflect a different feature of society and to facilitate the realization of constitutional rights. A president, for example, is elected directly or indirectly by everyone and thereby summarizes society's general aspirations; each member of a parliament represents the interests of his or her constituents (geographic or otherwise); members of a federal chamber if the state is a federation represent the interests of the government's constituent parts – states, lands, republics, oblasts – and members of high courts, freed from excessive political control, search for those general principles we must follow if society is to be something more than a discordant mob.

It goes without saying that the ultimate constraint on the state derives from these different relations with society's ultimate sovereign, the people. However, this fact has been a source of great confusion and has resulted in the erroneous belief, discussed in an earlier chapter, that merely to vote is to be democratic. Because it is necessary to grant government the power to coerce us into doing things we might not otherwise do (for example, pay taxes), and because public officials can sometimes act before we can successfully challenge those actions, even a popularly elected state can threaten our liberties. Hence being democratic also requires that we construct a government whose parts will each check the excessive accumulation of power by its other parts and the illiberal actions that accompany such an accumulation. Thus:

> *Rule 30*: It is the combination of relationships between citizen and state and among the parts of the state and not just one of them that determines whether a political system can adjust ineffective policy, policy that undermines the rights posited in a constitution, and policy that might ultimately undermine the state's very stability.

The relation of different parts to the people gives those parts a different interest and thus ensures that they will not collude against the people; the relation of those parts to each other ensures that no one part and no single interest within society can dominate all the rest. Of course, Soviet constitutions provided for a variety of representative assemblies and courts. But, operating under the assumption that the Communist Party would know and would necessarily act in the interests of society, those constitutions set this fourth part of government above all others, without also giving the people any direct or meaningful control over its actions. Hence the label 'democratic socialism' was little more than a sham – the more appropriate label was simply 'authoritarianism'.

Democratic systems contrast sharply with this picture, since they place no part of the government in a superior position. Parliamentary systems make all parts initially subservient to the legislature by giving it strong powers of appointment and dismissal. But a check on these powers is provided by allowing a chief of state or prime minister to dissolve the legislature and to call for new elections, and by giving the courts independent authority to judge the constitutionality of the government's and parliament's actions. Presidential systems sometimes tolerate a less direct relation between voters and public officials (members of one legislative branch may be appointed by regional governments, and presidents may be elected indirectly through such devices as an electoral college), but they compensate by requiring a 'balance of power' among the different parts of government while giving each part a different relation to the people.

Since many of the successor states of the USSR will most likely implement some form of presidential government and since the undecided issue here is the relative powers of that office, it is useful to consider the construction of this balance. Briefly, balance is achieved by implementing a *separation of powers* among the three primary branches of government, where this separation is intended to ensure that the excesses of one branch can be checked by the other two. Thus if the president fails to execute the law, the court can direct the executive to act otherwise and the legislature can use its control of state revenues to do the same. If the court fails its responsibilities, the executive and the legislature, together, can influence (albeit slowly) the court's direction by their joint power of appointment. Finally, if the legislature itself performs poorly, the courts can refuse to enforce unconstitutional laws, whereas the president, in addition to vetoing legislative acts, can use the prestige of his office to bring public pressure to bear on the legislature.

These checks, however, point to a practical difficulty. A complete separation of powers is impossible – each branch must have an interest in, and some authority over, the other two. We cannot have legislatures treating issues that do not concern the courts or the executive; and, by definition, the courts and the executive must implement the laws legislatures pass. So a stable constitution must allow some overlap in the jurisdictions of each branch. But in designing this overlap, we create chaos if we allow too much, as when we give legislative power to the president or the courts, or executive power to the legislature (the current Russian constitution does this by proclaiming the president the protector of the constitution, by allowing him to issue decrees whenever the law is silent, and by empowering him to abrogate regional executive actions he deems unconstitutional). Much of the conflict we observe in states in which chief executives regularly battle their parliaments derives not merely from political ambition but from the fact that the powers of these two branches impact each other too greatly. Thus:

> *Rule 31*: Too much overlap, then, creates confusion; too little threatens autocracy. A stable constitution requires a balance between too much and too little joint authority and reciprocal power.

So what precisely is the optimal balance? Should the legislature, for example, have the power to influence or even dictate the selection of the heads of ministries? Should the president be empowered to dissolve the legislature rather than merely being empowered to veto legislation? Should members of a Supreme or Constitutional Court be subject to periodic review and reappointment? These questions are not easily answered, but our prejudice is for overlap to be minimized and kept just great enough to ensure against the dominance of any one branch of government. In this event, each branch must act more responsibly, because it is less able to blame its failings on the actions of others. And with focused responsibilities, each branch becomes more amenable to control by the primary relationship a constitution establishes: the relationship between government and the people.

Presidential government aside, the point we want to emphasize is that all politics proceeds in accordance with rules, and by careful constitutional draftsmanship, we can coordinate political élites, as well as the rest of us, to the rules of democracy. The task of draftsmanship, however, is to devise rules to which we can all adhere – rules that no set of individuals has the means and the incentive to upset and that are themselves in balance. In the words of James Madison (*Federalist Papers*):

> In framing a government that is to be administered by men over men, the great difficulty lies in this: you must first enable the government to control

the governed; and in the next place oblige it to control itself. A dependence of the people is, no doubt, the primary control on the government; but experience has taught mankind the necessity of auxiliary precautions.

It is the absence of these precautions – the absence of a power that could offset that of the party or of the autocrat – that led to the conclusion that Soviet constitutions had 'failed'; it is the presence of these precautions that gives stable democracies their character.

10. Constitutions: Are There Rules for How to Write Them?

Because both the '36 and '77 Soviet constitutions embodied a concept of government that was inherently flawed and incapable of securing proclaimed rights and social guarantees, the unsatisfactory performance of these documents does not indicate the infeasibility of constitutional democracy in an ex-communist state. Nevertheless, few readers are likely to be convinced by that argument alone or led to the view that they ought to pay any attention to any constitution's content. Rather than concern themselves with political issues that occur at some rarefied level of power in Moscow, Kiev, Tashkent or Minsk, most people are understandably preoccupied with personal matters. A few may find ways to prosper, but the majority of the population in an economy undergoing wrenching transformation must be concerned with simple survival. Such circumstances are hardly ones that place arguments about new constitutions at centre stage.

But even if worrying about politics cannot put food on tables or shoes on feet, the design of a new constitution and the manoeuvres of political élites over its content warrant attention if only because of a constitution's role in a democracy. A constitution is not a piece of paper that, once written, can be filed away in some drawer, to be used by public officials as a justification for their actions and as a basis for securing political advantage over opponents. It ought to be a statement of society's highest political values and preferred forms of political organization. Constitutions are not prepared to give legitimacy to some predetermined governmental structure or to justify the actions of any particular faction in the government. They are written so people can organize and coordinate themselves to political purpose. Many of the things we want out of life – good schools, a prosperous economy, public safety – cannot be realized without coordinated social action. A written constitution is one of the things we must have if we are to rule ourselves and decide the government's role, if any, in the realization of those ends.

Primitive villages and tribes organized themselves through custom and tradition by accepting the leadership of elders and hereditary chieftains. Later, people gave their sanction (not always voluntarily) to kings and monarchs who may have ruled in their personal interest but who were expected to coordinate their subjects for some common purpose: even kings need a reasonably prosperous realm if there are to be things to tax. Communist ideology rejected the idea of the divine right of kings but, following earlier tradition, substituted the dictatorship of the party for that of the autocrat. People in a democracy reject the idea that any single individual or part of society has the right to rule. We seek to rule ourselves. However, self-rule does not materialize automatically merely by asserting a desire for it. It requires that we carefully construct some aids that were unnecessary when the power of the state was in the hands of an autocrat or a self-appointed oligarchy.

The nature of those aids is determined, first, by the fact that we must accept the idea that there will always be disagreements and honest differences of opinion as to how best to achieve social ends. There will also be honest disagreements over the ends themselves. We make no assumption of unanimity over anything except for the idea that people prefer to proceed peacefully as long as doing so promises them, their family and their friends a reasonably rewarding life. The character of those aids is determined also by the fact that we cannot try to reinvent procedures for resolving conflict every time we are called upon to make a decision. This approach – not too dissimilar from what currently characterizes politics in many states – leads to endless debate over the methods for making decisions, over the method for making decisions about methods of making decisions, and so on.

Of all the aids we might construct, none is more important than a constitution. This is the principal device whereby we coordinate our actions so as to select some set of rules and procedures for making social decisions. A constitution accomplishes these tasks in three ways:

1. It lists those basic values (rights) that are to remain unquestioned throughout our political debates.
2. It defines the domain of government and the relations of different levels of government to each other.
3. It prescribes the rules of political process, the rules whereby we select our leaders, and the ways in which those leaders are to organize themselves to serve us.

Thus the writing and adoption of a constitution is the ultimate act of democratic social self-organization and coordination.

Of course, it is not unreasonable for people to remain sceptical about a piece of paper and to ask: 'how can we ever hope to enforce its provisions when abiding by a written democratic constitution is not part of our tradition or culture?'. If there is a tradition, this argument continues, it is that of having constitutions enforced by an autocrat or, as in the Soviet case, by a tyrant.

Admittedly, trying to understand how a democratic constitution is enforced seems difficult. Such a document cannot be enforced by a legislature, a chief executive or the courts, since it is the constitution itself that defines the rules under which these parts of the government operate. If they have the ultimate power of enforcement, then they also have the power to change a constitution to suit their purposes. This is not to say that we do not hope to create institutions that make it in the self-interest of politicians to act to honour the provisions of a constitution. But seeing this as the ultimate source of constitutional stability merely pushes the problem back a step so that we must then ask: 'who enforces the provisions of a constitution that establish and define the self-interest of politicians?'.

In fact if there is a higher authority in a democracy and an ultimate source of enforcement, it can only be the people themselves. If constitutions are to guide our political deliberations and if they are to restrict our political leaders to act in our interest, then the people must consensually agree to abide by a constitution's terms. If the people are unwilling to act in accordance with it and to sanction those who fail to do so, then no special words, clauses, edicts, decrees or governmental forms will do the job for them. There is no precise relationship between a president and the legislature or between national government and regional governments that will guarantee constitutional stability. A constitution serves its purpose and endures only if the people – voters, soldiers, civil servants and public officials – are willing to abide by it and if they believe that others will do the same.

A constitution can accomplish this task in only one way: it must become a part of society's moral and spiritual fabric. As we argued earlier, acting 'constitutionally' must become equivalent to acting in accordance with other social norms, such as respecting and honouring one's parents, abiding by one's sense of patriotism or aiding strangers in peril. The 'trick' of democratic transition, then, is finding a way through public debate and through trial and error to render constitutional principles a part of our thinking about legitimate political process. Once this is done, a constitution's enforcement becomes a self-fulfilling prophecy.

We understand that this argument may seem utopian. Shouldn't we first get the economy functioning in some minimal way, even if that requires temporary autocratic rule, since only then can we begin to see what forms of political organization are best suited to our purposes? And even if we are forced to begin thinking about a constitution, shouldn't we leave the determination of things to specialists since we have had so little experience with democracy?

The answer to both questions should be no. We can take up again our earlier argument that democratic rules, especially those set forth in a constitution, are like the social norms that regulate and coordinate our day-to-day relations with people, in order to offer some general guidelines for writing and evaluating written constitutions. Because these suggestions apply regardless of whether the country in question adopts a presidential or a parliamentary system, regardless of whether the state is unitary or federal, and regardless of what choices are made with respect to the myriad of other decisions that go into the construction of a constitution, people can use these rules to evaluate any draft proposal set before them:

> *Rule 32*: Social norms do not arise from a single source – they are 'there' as part of custom and tradition. Similarly, just as no part of the government can be the exclusive guardian of a constitution's content, none can be the master of changes to it.

Allowing any part of the government the exclusive right to amend a constitution threatens instability. So when designing the procedures under which such a document can be amended, even if we choose to require the involvement of our legislature (since it is an important repository of relevant expertise and a valuable forum for debating the wisdom of any change), we should also involve the people directly (through referenda) or indirectly (via the acceptance of change by regional and republic governments). Social norms work because they are 'generally accepted' – constitutions and constitutional changes work the same way. Next:

> *Rule 33*: Social norms sustain themselves only if people expect others to abide by them and if they anticipate sanctions when they fail to do so, but doing so is impossible if they are confusing or poorly understood. Hence a

constitution should not be drafted with the idea that it will be a tool of lawyers. Long, convoluted clauses of uncertain meaning undermine constitutional stability; brevity is essential.

Plain language of common meaning provides a surer protection for society and a more effective device for coordinating opposition to those who would violate the spirit of a constitution than any number of clauses replete with concerns for extraordinary contingencies. Third:

> *Rule 34*: Social norms are simply stated. Similarly, we should resist elaborate statements of rights that give the appearance of making those rights immediately enforceable, since doing so merely compounds the problem of enforcement by adding additional layers to the document that require interpretation and legislation.

The temptation, regrettably common, is to view constitutions as contracts that seek to leave nothing to chance. But just as contracts can only be enforced by a higher authority, writing a constitution in this form tempts us to begin a futile search for the philosopher-king or to the dangerous creation of the dictator. People must instead begin placing their faith in the representative institutions and courts that a constitution establishes. Next:

> *Rule 35*: Norms are practical, and do not require that people do impossible things. A constitution should not be obscured by utopian requirements that the state accomplish things that may or may not be feasible.

There are policies we may want the state to pursue – protecting retired or disabled persons from poverty, providing for a viable system of education, ensuring an ample and affordable supply of housing. But a constitution should focus on the institutions and rights that are sufficient to ensure society's ability to coordinate for the realization of policy goals as expressed through democratically elected legislatures, governors and presidents. Fifth:

> *Rule 36*: Social norms guide our lives because we can all recognize the actions that violate them. Thus, it serves little purpose to assert in a constitution, for example, that 'the highest value is man and his life, liberty, honour and dignity', because such provisions do not direct the state to anything in particular.

Next:

Rule 37: A social norm is limited in scope. Similarly, constitutions add to society's social organization only in the limited domain of politics.

Including requirements that children care for their parents, that parents care for their children or that people care for the environment and for their cultural heritage are out of place in such a document. Other norms of social behaviour will attend to such matters – a constitution is not the place to attempt to structure all of society. Seventh:

Rule 38: Social norms are adaptable and timeless. A constitution should have the same character.

It may be difficult to avoid paying special attention to immediate problems – housing, ethnic conflict, inflation, and so on. But if we focus too strongly on the resolution of contemporary problems, we are unlikely to generate a document of lasting value. Instead a constitution seeks to create a set of institutions that will direct the resolution of all problems, both in the present and those that cannot be anticipated.

This last rule is especially difficult to follow, because nearly everyone will try to assess the immediate implications of a new constitution for their own welfare. This occasions a problem illustrated by card players who must choose the game they will play. If they choose before the cards are dealt, different players may hold different preferences, depending on which game best matches their beliefs about their comparative advantages in skill. But agreement should be possible, especially if each values the mere pleasure of playing. On the other hand, if they must choose after the cards are dealt, each person will prefer a game that makes his hand a likely winner Agreement will be reached only if the players allow their long-term interests to overcome their short-term ones. The situation is not much different in the transition to democracy. Although we may prefer to redeal the cards, this alternative is not wholly practical; and for most of us the cards have already been dealt. So each of us must somehow overcome our short-term concerns and try, as best we can, to look to the future. Unfortunately, there is no guarantee that people can or will do this. But we can offer one practical suggestion: write a minimal document that focuses only on the bare essentials of institutional design and that as much as possible leaves the ultimate resolution of specific policy issues up to, if not chance, at least to the skill of the players who play. In this way, players of the game of democracy will have an incentive to become skilled, which, in the long run, can only increase their commitment to the game.

11.   Federalism: Ingredient for Stability or a Recipe for Dissolution?

Included in the list of pressing needs for ostensibly federal states such as Russia and Ukraine is a solution to internal ethnic and linguistic conflicts that at the same time create incentives for each state's separate parts to remain within their federations. There are three commonly discussed paths to this end. The first is force applied by a resurrected authoritarian state. We realize that a deteriorating economy has led more than a few people to believe that democracy exacerbates problems and that an increasing number of people point to China as an example of successful economic reform directed by a centralized, authoritarian state. But people, in addition to wanting to live in stable and prosperous states, also demand their individual rights and liberties. Hence before any coercive route is chosen and before any element of the ex-USSR once again travels the path favoured by extremists of both the Right and the Left, we need to explore the democratic institutions that might help resolve regional conflicts.

Quite understandably, a good number of leaders in the political capitals of the world argue that a stable democracy requires placing most power in the hands of a central government. Although regional and local governments might be afforded some degree of autonomy, their position relative to the national government should be negotiated on a case-by-case basis in such a way that the national government maintains the upper hand in these negotiations. In this view, a federation that accedes to regional demands for political and economic autonomy is little more than a recipe for the eventual dissolution of the country. Yugoslavia, for example, dissolved with decentralization and federalism seems incapable of providing any solution to Nigeria's ethnic–tribal problems.

However, aside from the possibility that there are engineering problems without solutions, a centralized democratic state is itself sometimes an unrealizable goal. National governments are often too weak to enforce central control even in ordinary matters such as tax collection.

Attempts to impose control can lead to further resistance on the part of regional authorities and to increased pressures for authoritarian methods. Here, then, we want to see how to construct a federalism that avoids these problems and that results in a stable democracy. After all, we cannot yet reject the hypothesis that Yugoslavia dissolved not merely because of decentralization, but because it implemented this idea in the wrong way. First, however, we need to divide our discussion into two parts: the formal, constitutional structure of a federal state and those 'informal' structures (for example, political parties) that arise to organize and direct political action. This chapter focuses on constitutional structures; later ones examine parties and the special role they play in ensuring a political system's stability.

We begin by first dispensing with the idea that the fragility of, say, Russia or Ukraine, derives mostly from economic problems. It is true that with an economy in free-fall, each region and district seeks to control the resources in its territory. Such is the explanation for the USSR's dissolution and for the problems of the Commonwealth of Independent States (CIS). But economics provides only a partial explanation of the centrifugal forces operating today. The depression of the 1930s impacted on everyone, yet only a few countries experienced revolutionary political change. The forces working today against the stability of Canada cannot be described as the consequences of severe economic dislocation – any of the successor states of the USSR would love to have Canada's economic 'problems'. Nigeria's economic problems are more the consequence of political instability than a cause of it. And few could argue that the USSR's dissolution was collectively economically rational – the motives of national leaders who sought to consolidate their power overcame any notion of collective economic rationality.

The fact is that disputes and competition between regional and national governments, as well as among regional governments, are ubiquitous and eternal. No one prefers to be taxed by a distant government; everyone prefers to control whatever they have or hope to have; national governments always prefer to increase their power; and regional authorities always resist the supremacy of national officials while at the same time seeking advantage whenever possible over other regions. The American Civil War did not end the dispute between state and national governments; Switzerland's cantons continue to compete against the national government for supremacy; and members of the European Community continue to struggle against the interests of the Community as a whole and against each other. Economic turmoil may exacerbate conflicts, but our task is to see if a well-designed federalism can moderate the effects of that turmoil.

So if we cannot eliminate national–regional competition, how do we control its effects? To answer this question we begin by viewing the national government as a referee that coordinates regions to do those things they cannot do separately in any reasonably efficient way – provide for the national defence, coin money, ensure the obligation of contracts, ensure free trade within the federation, and so on. But in constructing a federal state we must guard against two things: (1) competition among regions that would upset the federal balance; and (2) a national government that usurps power at the expense of the regions so as to drag things back in the direction of a unitary centralized state in which it is no longer possible to realize the benefits of decentralization. The first of these, illustrated by Yugoslavia, Nigeria and possibly Canada, can in a self-evident way result in political instability and the dismemberment of a state; the second can do the same to the extent that any increase in the power of the national government only increases the incentives of regional governments to go their own way, even to secede.

An important, even necessary, protection against the first possibility is the construction of a federation that avoids giving to some regions a different relation to the national government than is given to other parts of the federation. A federal system that is not symmetric – one in which degrees of autonomy vary from one region to another and in which a confusing array of bilateral and multilateral treaties characterize the state's organization – is untenable. One region's greater autonomy legitimizes demands for greater autonomy by other regions. In the asymmetric federalism, regions compete for special favours, for particular dispensations from central control and for recognition of their 'unique circumstances'. And it is the escalation of these demands, brought about by the general inequality of condition, that is the chief threat to the stability of any federal state.

This competition among political subunits requires that the national government be involved continuously in the allocation of differential benefits, with the inevitable result that some sub-parts will seek to win control of the national government and use its power for their own ends. Thus one key rule for creating a durable federation is this:

> *Rule 39*: No federal subject should have any more or less autonomy than any other part. No region should be singled out as having characteristics

that justify making its residents any less or more democratically free than people elsewhere.

Indeed, if there is reason to grant special autonomous rights to one region, that reason should apply to all regions equally.

Symmetric or otherwise, a national government will find it difficult to maintain the autonomy of federal subjects. All politicians seek power, and those who would lead a national government are no different than the rest. Thus another rule of federal state construction is:

> *Rule 40*: Maximize the autonomy of federal subjects by reserving for the national government only those functions it alone can perform (for example, maintenance of a national defence, maintenance of a stable currency, guaranteeing the free flow of goods, services and people across the different parts of the republic, and the establishment of a court system that provides for equal treatment before the law for all citizens).

This rule is supported by two facts. First, people learn to be democratic, to value rights, and to organize to press their demands on the state by learning how to organize and participate in local and regional politics. People will pay only slight attention to things they cannot influence and that influence them only indirectly. And they will be most cynical about processes that seem beyond their control. Local and regional matters should be otherwise; indeed local and regional politics should be the great classroom of democratic ideas and values. Democratic values are not learned by the exhortations of political and intellectual élites. They are learned by the practical experience that participation in local and regional politics provides. But this classroom cannot exist if local and regional governments have little control over those things that affect them and that do not affect other regions. It cannot exist if political élites in a national capital insist on appointing regional governors; it cannot exist if they insist on directing the design of local and regional governments (aside from ensuring that they are democratic); it cannot exist if they insist on deciding everything from local speed limits and school textbooks to the methods whereby local and regional officials are elected. These are the things that must be decided by people who are perfectly capable of making their own judgements about the things that most concern them.

The other fact that supports this last rule is that conflicts within a political subunit are less likely to disrupt national politics in a decentralized system than in a centralized one. All conflicts in the centralized state must be resolved by central authorities because only they, by definition, have the power to act. A decentralized federalism, in contrast, allows people to search first for local solutions, because doing so maintains their autonomy. Only when internal compromises cannot be achieved should the national government be called into the conflict to umpire a resolution. And the fewer conflicts we move up to the national level, the fewer conflicts we allow to threaten the state's ultimate stability. This fact as much as any other justifies Thomas Jefferson's assertion that, 'the government that governs best is the government that governs least'. This assertion is not a call for anarchy; it merely recognizes the fact that the dead hand of bureaucratic centralization leads to bureaucratic insensitivities to local and regional needs. This dead hand stifles innovation and experimentation with policy and it eliminates any incentives for local and regional authorities to take responsibility for their actions.

Rule 40, however, does not provide much practical guidance in the construction of a stable democratic federation, and thus we should ask: what are a national government's essential functions? We cannot, of course, list everything here, but again taking up the view of a national government as referee among, and coordinator of, regional governments, minimally it should be empowered to:

- prohibit restraint of trade across regions, since otherwise regional governments will seek to advantage industries within their border by taxing or regulating the free flow of goods and services;
- ensure that contracts agreed to in one region are enforceable in all regions, since we cannot allow people to escape their obligations by moving from one region to another;
- regulate the money supply, since it is best positioned to oversee macro-economic policy;
- provide for a national defence, since regional governments may not respond appropriately to external threats; indeed they will be tempted to provide only for their own defence and internal security;
- regulate environmental matters that impact several regions simultaneously whenever these regions act to pass environmental costs off to neighbours.

Even this abbreviated list requires one additional constitutional provision. Specifically, a national government cannot perform its coordinative function unless the constitution:

- establishes the supremacy of federal law over regional and local laws and defines the issue domains for the application of this principle.

Although the idea of supremacy is likely to be strongly resisted by regional governments, without such a constitutional clause the national government cannot establish a common economic market within its borders, cannot ensure the obligation of contracts, and cannot compel the different parts of society to contribute to the national defence. In short, without the supremacy of federal law, the national government cannot perform its essential functions.

The final issue that concerns us with respect to constitutional matters is the legitimate concern in Moscow and Kiev, as well as capitals elsewhere, that if left to their own devices, regional élites will take advantage of their isolation to subvert democratic process in their regions, either by engaging in wholesale fraud or by otherwise infringing on the constitutional rights of minorities in their regions. If democracy in a large republic functions because no interest or faction can form a permanent majority, then we need also to recognize the statistical fact that permanent (for example, ethnic) majorities are more likely in small political units than large ones. To protect against the abrogation of rights within regions, then, a democratic federal constitution should:

- guarantee to the citizens of each region a democratic form of government.

Although regions should be allowed to design governments that best suit their needs and traditions, including procedures for electing representatives to the national legislature, federal courts should have the authority to oversee matters so as to ensure that no one's constitutional rights are violated.

What we have said thus far may seem like a good deal of wishful thinking. On the one hand we have argued that those who would direct the destiny of any ex-communist state must unlearn the instinct to centralize; on the other hand it would appear that, especially with respect to a constitutional supremacy clause, we have given the central government a great deal of authority. Thus to the extent that there is no reason to suppose that mere words on paper can enforce anything, we have not yet responded fully to the question: what keeps a decentralized federalism decentralized and yet whole? What keeps the national government in a decentralized federalism from eventually usurping power? What keeps regional governments from coalescing against each other? And what ensures that we are not merely encouraging the ultimate dissolution of the state by deliberate decentralization? The responses to these questions require that we consider things other than mere constitutional guarantees and structures. We must also look at the form and operation of those organizations that people establish to influence political outcomes – political parties. The role of parties in a federal state, then, is the subject of our next chapter.

12. Political Parties: A Source of Faction or Agents of Stability?

In the previous chapter we argued that any state choosing to be a federation should grant as much autonomy as possible to its sub-parts and should treat those parts equally. However, we concluded with some unanswered questions concerning the overall stability of a federation and the maintenance of the federal bargain between the centre and federal subjects.

Political stability and the maintenance of that bargain are intimately connected. If federal subjects lose autonomy so that the political system moves in the direction of simple majority rule, minorities – especially territorial ethnic ones – are more likely to feel, and to be, disadvantaged. However, constitutional restrictions on a national government are, as much as anything else, subject to reinterpretation and manipulation. Giving regional governments control over some resource does not stop the national government from adjusting its taxation and regulation policies so as to circumvent the restrictions placed on it. Giving an ethnic group the right to educate its children in the language of its choice does not stop a government from imposing contrary requirements by nationalizing the funding of education and by creating onerous restrictions on what is required for a share of those funds.

Guarding against such possibilities with additional constitutional guarantees merely makes that document less enforceable. We cannot keep elaborating guarantees of autonomy. Doing so merely avoids the problem of determining how the last added clause, prohibition or requirement is to be enforced. More problematical is the fact that negotiating the precise terms of autonomy – deciding within the context of a constitution which matters fall under the jurisdiction of the national government and which belong to regional or district governments – is generally a protracted and contentious process that exacerbates conflict. As the dispute between Quebec and the rest of Canada illustrates, such negotiations can set region against region as each claims special privilege or fears that such privilege will be given to others.

These concerns are not arguments against constructing a decentralized federalism. After all, this approach is credited with being Switzerland's source of stability despite its linguistic cleavages, as well as an important component of America's stability despite its ethnic and geographic heterogeneity. But neither Switzerland nor the United States confronts economic problems of a type that pervade the territory of the Soviet Union. So even if we accept the idea that meaningful grants of regional autonomy are an essential part of a stable democratic state, we should ask whether there are ways to establish these grants without threatening dissolution, whether we can put in place a process whereby autonomous rights can be renegotiated without exacerbating conflicts, and whether this process can be designed to resist the forces that act to undermine any plan of decentralization and fairness.

Because the terms of federation set forth in a constitution must be self-enforcing, we must look to those extra-constitutional processes and the incentives of political élites that, although influenced by a constitution, act to undermine or to re-enforce its provisions. And of all the extra-constitutional things that emerge in a democracy that both shape and are shaped by the motives of political élites, nothing is more important than the political party. Until we describe and understand the role of parties, we cannot predict how any system will function and whether it will in fact be stable.

Political parties in a liberal democracy are not personal factions or social clubs designed to express one ideological position or another as loudly as possible. Parties are the things politicians use to get elected: to mobilize voters, to communicate their issue positions, to raise campaign funds and to organize legislative coalitions. But just as politicians and political structure influence the form and role of parties in a democracy, parties influence the actions of politicians. Directly or indirectly, they influence the incentives of candidates to negotiate compromises, and they determine which issues become salient in national elections and which ones are relevant only at local level.

To see, then, how parties contribute to federal stability, let us consider what lessons America provides. We realize that some people might object that, given its different traditions and economic circumstances, and given its absence of territorial ethnic groups, America is irrelevant to places such as Russia, Ukraine, and so on. However, America is not only a stable federalism, it is also one that experienced civil war in the last century. The sources of its stability and instability, then, may illustrate some general possibilities. In particular, America offers some important lessons about how some constitutional provisions in addition to those discussed earlier, facilitate stability, but that, until we examine the structure of political parties, might go unappreciated.

Since threats to regional autonomy are a precursor to instability, our focus is on discovering how federal subjects maintain their autonomy despite the authority we give to a national government, including the requirement that its laws be supreme. Turning, then, to the American experience, we can trace the ability of states there to oppose successfully the encroachments of the national government on to the structure of America's two major parties, which derives from the influence of four elements of the national constitution:

1. The requirement that national legislators – members of the House of Representatives and the Senate – be residents of their constituencies.
2. The flexibility it gives state governments (which have the right to design republican governments to their own liking) to prescribe the manner of election of national representatives (subject to the condition that those procedures be 'democratic').
3. The absence of any device (such as the authority to dissolve the legislature) that allows the president to control legislative parties or even the party he nominally heads.
4. The method of presidential election, which requires national support that transcends regional appeals.

These four points take us a long way in explaining the most evident feature of America's national parties: they are highly decentralized organizations that compete with seemingly obscure non-ideological platforms. In fact America does not have two *national* parties – it has 50 Republican and 50 Democratic *state* parties (more, since state parties are themselves coalitions of local organizations) that act every four years to compete for the presidency, but that otherwise function to compete for state and local offices. Hence national legislators are elected according to rules set by their states (including the geographic definition of their districts) and as part of campaigns run by local organizations. Consequently, these legislators, even if they seek national office or otherwise aspire to national and international visibility, cannot ignore local needs. And with a president who can influence their electoral destinies only slightly, that office provides only the weakest incentive to form strong national party organizations.

These facts mean that national legislators remain protective of local and regional concerns. But these facts do not explain why coalitions do not form on the basis of purely regional concerns. Part of the explanation is the absence of marked territorial differences – ethnicity that correlates with geography, for example. But in addition to this fortuitous circumstance, the danger of legislative and party coalitions organized on a purely regional basis is avoided because of the importance of the presidency and the way that office is filled. Parties outside the legislature and factions in it cannot ignore the importance of winning this office, and it is the quest for the presidency rather than purely geographic interests that is the primary basis for party structures in and out of the legislature.

That only two parties form and that the legislature organizes around two primary blocks labelled 'Democrat' and 'Republican' follows from the rules of presidential elections. Without examining details or the history of why it is so, the 'winner-takes-all' character of those rules and the limited opportunities they provide for minor parties to block the election of a winner compels politicians to coalesce into two blocks: Democrat and Republican. And insofar as regional coalitions are concerned, those laws give parties an incentive to make geographically broad appeals. Once a party wins a majority of votes in a state, it wins all of that state's electoral votes and increasing its vote there further serves no purpose. Thus rather than increase its vote in any state to the greatest extent possible, if it is reasonably certain of winning there, a party directs its remaining resources at states that are more competitive. Thus although local concerns and characteristics may give one party or another an advantage in specific states, Democrats and Republicans will compete across most geographic regions, thereby making those parties national.

Because they must compete nationally for the presidency, both parties must attempt to form coalitions that encompass a broad range of interests by negotiating a wide variety of issues internally. Thus even though local concerns remain dominant within parties, the quest for the presidency compels them to resolve innumerable conflicts internally before those conflicts bubble up to disrupt national politics. The one instance in which geographic conflict was negotiated outside of party structures led ultimately to civil war, which occurred when politicians short-circuited the natural process of intra-party compromise and upset a delicate constitutional balance by artificially maintaining a Senatorial representation of southern slave states equal to that of the north. Because this arrangement could not be sustained on moral and practical grounds (the practical matter being the predominance of northern industrial development), and because it was set in the context of a debate (since resolved) over the supremacy of federal law, it led to a split of one of the national parties and, subsequently, to a war between north and south.

So the primary guarantor of the autonomy of state governments and the primary obstacle to inter-regional conflict is not prosperity (which may be more the consequence of stability as its cause) or any explicit constitutional protection of autonomy. Rather it is a consequence of a delicate constitutional balance formed by a complex combination of provisions that lead to a decentralization of party structures but that compel parties to negotiate their internal contradictions as they search for ways to form winning national coalitions.

These devices may have been arrived at as much by accident as by planning (the framers of the American constitution failed to appreciate fully the role parties would play in their future). And we certainly have not argued that the internal conflicts of today's ethnically heterogeneous states are less divisive than those that confronted America in the 1850s. But the operation of these devices provides important lessons for those who would design a new federalism for, say, Russia or Ukraine. Political parties can unify as well as divide, and constitutional structures need to accommodate this fact. We should not look to any single clause or provision to accomplish our goal of stability – party structures and roles are determined by the interplay of many things. Looking at a single relationship, such as the relative powers of a president versus the legislature, will lead to unanticipated consequences.

Many things do distinguish America from any other state. Most important is the fundamental difference in the composition of ethnic group demands in America and states such as Russia or Ukraine. Owing to the structure of their economies, there is considerably less geographic mobility within these states and a good deal more territorial conflict. Combined with an economic deterioration that precludes an explicit or implicit process of 'buying off' these demands, compromise seems unrealizable. We cannot argue, then, that a properly designed federal system, with compatible election laws, will solve all the problems associated with ethnicity, language and religion. We can only argue that things should not be made worse by an inappropriate choice of institutional structure.

A second difference concerns the possibility that a state will choose to have a parliamentary rather than a presidential system. Much of what we have said about America requires that its regional parties have a strong incentive to coalesce to win the presidency. Without this incentive, inter-regional compromises would be more difficult (even impossible) to negotiate outside of the legislature. Thus the issue of a strong versus a weak president cannot be divorced from plans to ensure that a federal structure remain in place and that inter-ethnic compromises be encouraged. Until and unless proponents of a governmental form that emphasizes the power of parliament over that of a president can tell us how their federal structure will survive, we should remain prejudiced towards the establishment of a strong president – at least one capable of vetoing legislation and directing the operation of the executive branch of government. This is not to say that parliamentary government and meaningful federalism are incompatible, only that federalism is more difficult to sustain without the focus that presidential elections provide.

Returning now to the structure of parties in a federation, we have thus far focused on the features of the national constitution that engender decentralized parties. There are, however, some requirements that must be met by regional and local governments themselves. Specifically:

> *Rule 41*: The governments of federal subjects should make broad use of direct election not only for local and regional legislatures, mayors and governors, but for other public offices as well.

It might seem unproductive to follow this rule. After all, we cannot assume that many voters will have good information about a great many, if any, of the candidates for these offices. Thus we might ask: doesn't direct election open the door to the election of people who are merely adept at manipulating public opinion? Indeed a positive answer to this question is not unreasonable, and was not an uncommon opinion in the formative years of the United States. Whatever the benefits of widespread application of elections, they were not universally appreciated in the first quarter of the 19th century. But what are those benefits and, in particular, what is the relevance of the pervasive use of elections at the regional and local level to the character of federalism? Briefly, the benefits take three interdependent forms. First, pervasive use of elections at the state and local level facilitates the formation of state and local party organizations that become the building blocks for federal, national parties. In this way, then, local and regional elections begin the process of party formation that is essential to a stable democracy.

Second, application of Rule 41 strengthens national parties and integrates them with local and regional ones. It might seem that regional elections would only encourage the rise of regional parties and political élites which would act in competition with the national government and which, for their own purposes, would raise issues that would threaten political stability. This is sometimes true, but primarily in countries in which regional competition focuses on a single salient office such as governor. Consider, though, the candidate for local judge in New York City who, during one of Franklin Roosevelt's presidential campaigns, gave his campaign funds to the local Democratic Party in anticipation of professional assistance (as reported by Samuel Lubell in *The Future of American Politics*, 1954). Weeks went by, but he saw nothing – no posters or radio broadcasts that mentioned his name! Agitated and uneasy, he returned to party headquarters to complain. The head of the party took him to the southern tip of Manhattan where the ferry from Staten Island landed and, as a ferry pulled in, he pointed to the floating debris and garbage that swirled at the ferry's stern, towed by its wake, and said, 'the name of your ferry is Franklin Delano Roosevelt'. Thus in an election in which voters confront scores of candidates about whom they know little or nothing, the essential commodity possessed by candidates is their partisan labels and the fact that these labels are shared by viable candidates for national office. Extensive application of direct election at the local and state level, then, gives party leaders a valuable commodity with which to deal – the party's nomination and official sanction – which in turn gives those leaders an incentive to integrate their party with the national one. Moreover, the connection works in the other direction as well. While the name Roosevelt and the label 'Democrat' doubtlessly helped the local candidate for judge and countless other Democratic candidates for office, the organizations erected to nominate and facilitate local and state elections become an essential part of any national candidate's campaign. Thus in a symbiotic relationship, local and national parties rely on each other for their survival and success.

Finally, extensive application of direct elections gives those with political ambition a ready means of moving up the ladder of political position and a home to those who would compete for the next rung. Moreover, because it is only natural to recruit candidates for national office from among those who have demonstrated effectiveness at campaigning and governing at the local or regional level, it ensures that those who achieve national office have a strong genetic connection to local and regional parties and governments.

13. Legislatures: Can They Govern Us If They Cannot Govern Themselves?

Legislators scream epithets, someone pushes someone else, and soon a group charges the lectern, reaching, grabbing and punching. Does this sound like the old People's Congress of Russia before its dissolution or the legislature of any of the newly formed successor states of the Soviet Union? Perhaps. But this scene could just as easily describe Japan's Diet or Taiwan's Yuan (where not only punches but also chairs, microphones and desks occasionally fly through the air). Such events are not uncommon; indeed in the early years of the US Congress many legislators attended sessions armed with pistols, and as late as 1856 one of them, Charles Sumner, was beaten senseless on the floor of the Senate by the nephew of an irate political opponent.

Of course, the dangers of incompetence and conflict seem greatest when legislative 'misbehaviour' occurs in a country with nuclear weapons that must make a painful transition from an authoritarian, centrally planned state to a liberal democratic, free enterprise one. Legislative incoherence threatens that transition because it threatens the things society needs most: a well-functioning judicial system, a clear body of contract and property law, and attention to the macro-economic policies of the state.

Insofar as the causes of this incoherence or misbehaviour are concerned, there are those who believe that legislatures in Russia and elsewhere behave as they do because so many legislators are merely 'warmed over' communists or *apparatchiks*, unable to comprehend the failure of their ideology and unwilling to give up any of the benefits they enjoyed under the previous regime. And there are those who see misbehaviour among even democratic reformers and who attribute it to naïveté and inexperience with their new-found ideology of liberal democracy and capitalism.

These arguments may be correct. But they circumvent the root of the problem and they generate inappropriate, even dangerous, responses. One response, based on the idea that the legislature 'has the wrong people in it', is the one Yeltsin pursued when he forcefully dissolved the People's Congress and decreed new elections. However, as subsequent events revealed, there is no guarantee that this response produces a legislature that is much different than the old one. There is, in fact, little evidence that legislators in a new democracy – even ex-communist ones – act any more in accordance with some narrow definition of self-interest than do legislators in an established, stable democracy. Scandals of all types occur with some frequency everywhere.

A second response is to give more power to a single authority – a president or prime minister – by allowing that person to legislate by decree or to suspend constitutional rights. This approach assumes that legislative incoherence is a greater danger than dictatorship, and it thereby tolerates postponement or even termination of democratic reform. But while it is true that strong arguments can be made for the view that states experiencing radical economic transformation cannot function as 'normal' democracies and that a greater degree of central control is required to keep politics from becoming incoherent or violent, this argument fails to attack the root cause of the problem of legislative incoherence.

As with many other things that we have tried to understand in this monograph, the cause of legislative inefficiency, misbehaviour, or incoherence lies with incentives. Legislators fail to generate coherent law not because they lack ability, but because they do not yet have the incentives to do so, including the incentive to develop the internal organizational structures that facilitate coordination and compromise. This absence of appropriate incentives in turn derives from the fact that legislators in a newly formed democracy are unlikely to have yet felt the full force of the imperatives of running for *re-election*. Indeed some may have never even observed such an election, whereas others may have done so, but in an incoherent setting in which dozens of candidates competed for the same office and in which the relationship between voters' actions and campaign strategies and tactics were obscure.

Experience tells us that if there is anything that draws a politician's attention to his or her responsibilities, it is the prospect of competing in an election against someone who will publicly broadcast every personal flaw and every incorrect decision to anyone who will listen. Although the prospect of competitive elections may be frightening to most politicians, it brings order to legislative deliberations since legislators must now try to communicate to voters that they are acting in their interest. The absence of the electoral threat and inexperience with competitive elections, on the other hand, yields a fragmented legislative 'party' structure and a less coherent legislative process. Things labelled 'parties' typically are not parties at all, that is, organizations designed to present the electorate with alternative policies and programmes and to secure votes for those who compete under their labels. Instead they are largely protest groups, ideological cabals, special interest lobbies and personal factions designed to advance the careers of specific individuals. In the absence of the threat of competitive elections, there is little need for these 'parties' to coalesce, to negotiate seriously their differences or to act so that an electorate views them as offering responsible policy alternatives. In fact doing so is taken as a sign of weakness or a failure of leadership.

Political parties in 'mature' democracies are organized to win elections. They are the devices politicians use to organize support within their constituencies and to communicate to the electorate their policy predispositions and their commitment to a rule of law. Parties organize in this way because voters, concerned about more personal matters, have little reason to devote much time to learning which candidate best represents their interests. If forced to listen to every promise and every prescription for change, they are easily overwhelmed and confused. Ordinary citizens, then, look for cues as to how to vote, and one important cue is a candidate's party label. If a party label can be made to convey anything, including the integrity of those who run under it, voters will use these labels in deciding who to support. Parties that succeed in associating themselves with attractive policies and attractive candidates survive; all others eventually disappear or are relegated to the sidelines of political events. The imperatives of electoral competition, then, compel legislators to cultivate the labels under which they seek election and re-election, so that members of a party within parliament have an incentive to ensure that their actions are responsible and serve a clear purpose.

The absence of, or inexperience with, the immediate threat of competitive elections also impacts a legislature's internal structure and, correspondingly, the efficiency of its operation. Without such a threat there is little need to organize oneself to proceed efficiently in the public's interest. Instead committee structures and debates arise on an *ad hoc* basis, since the only compelling force is one's definition of patriotism, unguided personal ambition or whim.

This is not to say that such motivations cannot lead legislators to support correct policies. But democracies do not place their faith in the fortuitous or accidental selection of well-intentioned representatives. They place their faith instead in ensuring that legislators will be directed to organize themselves in our interest because to do otherwise would lead us to replace them in the next election. We should not suppose, then, that legislatures are organized to do 'good'. Instead they will organize themselves to serve their own self-interest – they will reveal their votes when it is in their interest to do so; they will vote by secret ballot when they fear that doing otherwise will be personally costly; they will use committees and subcommittees if doing so aids their re-election; they will service constituent complaints when failing to do so costs them electoral support; and they will consult experts when they might be sanctioned by voters for making ill-advised decisions. What we must do through constitutional design, then, is ensure that their self-interest parallels ours.

Competitive elections are the primary route to this end. They compel legislators, even those who seek merely to get re-elected without convictions about policy, to organize and act in ways that maximize their chances of survival. If we have designed our electoral and representative mechanisms well, legislators will, in developing a structure that best suits their purposes, organize to serve our purposes.

Several practical suggestions follow from this somewhat cynical but not ill-founded perspective. First:

> *Rule 42*: Rather than try to specify the 'correct' organization of a legislature, constitutions should focus on clear specifications of modes of representation and electoral processes.

If a constitution tells legislators to organize in ways that do not serve their interests, they will find ways to operate differently. Constitutional provisions that require specific committees, ways of resolving disputes between legislative assemblies, and rules of procedure (except those that specify a quorum – the minimum number of legislators required to be present in order to conduct business – and those that specify special rules for considering constitutional amendments and impeachment) are generally unenforceable and are the first things to succumb to reinterpretation and amendment. In contrast:

> *Rule 43*: A clear specification of the timing of elections, term limits, when legislative sessions begin and end, and the basis of representation (by federal subject, by party-list proportional representation, by single-mandate district) lies at the heart of constitutional design.

Not everything dealing with representation or the details of election rules can be specified in a constitution. Issues such as campaign finance, the creation of authorities to administer elections, ballot forms, access to the media, the drawing of district boundaries, and so on can only be addressed by complex legislation. Discussing such issues in a constitution merely makes that document unwieldy and unenforceable. Thus the question arises as to who will oversee the creation and enforcement of electoral laws. Will local or regional governments have the opportunity to determine the rules under which they elect representatives or will these matters be dictated by some central authority, or even the legislature itself? Again, to strengthen federal relationships, our preference is for local determination of such matters. Indeed we prefer moving as much as possible out of the hands of those whose immediate fates are to be determined by such laws, since they will try to manipulate them to their own advantage.

That legislators will attempt to manipulate the rules of election so as to make their own positions more secure might make us ask how the things a constitution says about elections and representation can ever be enforced and remain stable. Why should electoral institutions dictate legislative structure and action rather than the other way around? What keeps those with power from manipulating election laws so that those laws exclusively serves only their interests?

In fact at least the broad outlines of election laws are enforceable for a simple reason: maintaining them will soon be in the self-interest of legislators themselves. Here another American example is instructive. It is generally accepted that America's method of electing a president has certain disadvantages, including the possibility that a popular vote winner will not be elected (as happened in 1824, 1876, 1888, arguably in 1960 and nearly in 1968). Hence the US Senate periodically considers various 'reforms'. But to date nothing much has changed, because no one is certain that any change will provide as sure a guarantee of a two-party system as does the current arrangement. However, one thing is certain: legislators who must decide any constitutional matter are winners at the game of two-party politics and they prefer to maintain that aspect of the game. Winners in any game rarely want to change its rules, since such changes threaten them with the prospect of becoming losers rather than winners. Rarely does the person winning at some card game suggest playing a different game; arguments for change come from the losers. And rarely does anyone winning at roulette move elsewhere in a casino. The same is true in politics. Thus to the extent that the courts and public opinion allow it, the American Republican and Democratic Parties collude to ensure that third-party candidates have as small a chance as possible at disturbing their competition. And since they are confident that current arrangements disadvantage third parties, those arrangements are largely unchallenged.

This discussion of how electoral laws become self-enforcing suggests a final rule, namely:

> *Rule 44*: The things a constitution says about representation and elections should be crafted carefully and in full appreciation of their long-term consequences.

It is too easy to write those parts of a constitution or even to draft initial legislation with an eye to securing immediate political advantage. However, it is in the long term that acts of statecraft are judged, not in the short term. And the long term is likely to be stable and prosperous only if those parts create the proper incentives among legislators.

14. A Two-Chamber Legislature: Isn't One More Than Enough?

Although some democratic states exist with only one legislative chamber, most have two. We should not be surprised, then, by the fact that despite their many differences, all draft constitutions prepared for the Russian Federation between 1991 and 1993 proposed to create both a lower chamber (now the State Duma) and an upper one (now the Federation Council). And following conventional democratic practice (as opposed to the idea of a Supreme Soviet elected by a larger assembly), all serious drafts proposed that each chamber be selected or elected independently of the other. However, in light of the disarray exhibited by legislators not only in Russia, but in even more established democracies, we are entitled to ask why two legislative chambers are needed when one provides all the entertainment we can tolerate. Wouldn't two chambers, each vying for power, only add to the confusion and to the possibility of executive–legislative or presidential–legislative stalemate? Why create more public officials than we already have? After all, public officials demand salaries, but they do not seem to yield a large return on this investment.

But before we use the alleged failings of any specific legislative body as a basis for predicting the consequences of new arrangements, we should first restate some arguments as to why the future need not be like the past. Recall our argument from the previous chapter that the character of legislative bodies such as the old People's Congress of Russia should not be attributed to the supposition that they are dominated by large numbers of unrepentant communists, entrenched *apparatchiks*, and faceless mediocrities. Legislators inherited from a dead regime may be of less than sterling character, but a legislature is not some simple arithmetic sum of the people in it. Instead the various Congresses and Soviets of the successor states of the USSR acted as they did (or act today as they do) because they came into being before anyone knew they were to be national rather than republic legislatures and because their members did not feel or otherwise fully appreciate the need to organize themselves into professional law-making institutions.

We understand that it might be difficult to imagine some members of any old Congress or Supreme Soviet becoming professional at much of anything (aside, perhaps, from how best to stymie reforms that might threaten the security of their positions). However, the differences between old and new legislatures will not come from some magical process that fills public office holders with wiser and more deliberative people. This difference will come, if it comes at all, from the ways in which legislators are compelled to represent national or local constituencies in their respective countries and to compete for public office in meaningful elections. With the prospect of regularly scheduled, competitive elections – an especially frightening idea for those who have never confronted such things – legislators will have to do more than scurry about whispering rumours of cabals, dividing and redividing into innumerable factions, or hatching plots against a government or a president. They will instead be forced to take *positive* action, to formulate policy, to draft legislation that confronts directly the innumerable problems their countries confront, to learn what it is their constituents want, and to anticipate what policies an election opponent might propose in attempting to unseat them. They will find it necessary to maintain permanent staffs, and to deliberate, hold committee meetings, gather data and vote. The mouthing of ideological generalities and personal insults will not wholly disappear, but they should subside, if only because legislators will fear an electorate that views them as unprofessional and unable to express and represent their views effectively.

Of course, what we have just said does not address the issue of a two-chamber legislature and does not answer two questions, both of which may be relevant to any state redesigning its governmental structure:

1. If a state already possesses a single legislative chamber (a Supreme Soviet or a Congress of People's Deputies), wouldn't it be simpler to 'improve' on what already exists by merely holding new elections and, if necessary, by clarifying the relationship of the legislature to the other parts of the state?

2. If a parliamentary system is chosen in which the authority to form and dismiss a government is to be held primarily by the 'lower' legislative branch, isn't an upper branch redundant?

So turning to the issue of legislative design, we note that there are two basic arguments for a two- rather than a single-chamber legislature:

1. Legislators *represent*, and there are different things that require representation.
2. Division of the legislature makes it more difficult for this branch to do stupid or dangerous things.

The first justification takes us to an important issue that will concern anyone who drafts a constitution. That issue is what it means to have 'fair' representation, and who it is that is to be represented – individual citizens, specific ethnic groups or the different geographic regions of a country.

How we address this issue depends on the nature of the country under consideration. If it is a small homogeneous state – Finland, Iceland or even Hungary – without salient regional or ethnic differences, then the issue of geographic or ethnic representation may not arise and the concept of 'fair' representation may be a simple thing: divide the country into any number of equally populous districts and let each district elect the same number of representatives to the relevant legislative chamber. This rule can admit a representation scheme in which the country is divided into as many districts as there are legislators and in which each deputy represents a specific district. Or, at the other extreme, it can admit a system in which the country consists of a single district and deputies are elected by party lists, where each party is awarded a proportion of seats in the legislature equal to its proportion of the popular vote. Some countries, such as Hungary, combine these two systems and elect approximately half of the legislature one way and half the other.

But suppose, for the moment, that we are dealing with a state such as Russia or Ukraine in which there is considerable variation in the economic interests of different parts of the country, or in which one ethnic group is predominant in one part of the country and another ethnic group predominant in some other part. Imagine that we implement the same formula for representation as we do in Finland, Iceland or Hungary. The difficulty now is that different geographic regions, although represented in proportion to their population, may argue and in fact believe that 'fair' representation requires that all specific interests or ethnicities be equally represented in the legislature regardless of their numbers in the population.

We accomplish little by trying to counter these views with debates about the meaning of fairness, since purely philosophical arguments are unlikely to dissuade people that the only practical protection against majority tyranny is representation based on something other than simple head counts. It is for this reason, then, that a second legislative chamber may be a practical necessity. By first dividing a country into specific constituencies defined by their geographic or ethnic character (or, in the case of, say, Russia or Ukraine, by taking pre-existing political subunits such as oblasts and republics), by requiring that all regions have identical representation in an upper legislative chamber and by making that chamber an integral part of the legislative process (for example, giving it a veto over any legislation), we have a system in which every region has an equal chance of blocking legislation it opposes: no region is any more or less pivotal than any other.

For federations, we compromise the principle of equal representation of people because forging a federation is like forming an alliance, and a two-chamber legislature is one of the compromises we make to achieve that end. It is important to note, however, that the meaning of this compromise should change over time. In societies with little geographic mobility and sharp, territorial ethnic divisions, this compromise may be one of the most important ones that we can make. But in a society with an advanced market economy and, correspondingly, with a mobile labour force, the meaning of geography (as well as of ethnicity) should diminish with time. Thus although the issue of big versus small states or urban versus rural played a significant role in the early years of the United States, mobility and the general homogenization of America leaves people there unconcerned about the fact that, as of 1994, the majority leader of the Senate came from a state (Maine) that ranked 38th in population among the 50 states, the minority leader came from a state (Kansas) that ranked 32nd, the Speaker of the House of Representatives came from a state (Washington) that ranked 18th, and the president had been governor of a state (Arkansas) that ranked 33rd.

What is a momentous compromise in one era can become irrelevant in another. However, making that compromise raises a number of subsidiary questions. Why, as is usually the case, do we make the upper chamber smaller than the lower one? Should the term lengths of deputies to the two chambers be the same or different? Should the powers of the two chambers be symmetric or asymmetric? Who will determine the rules under which elections to each chamber are conducted?

These questions cannot be addressed separately. We cannot choose, say, a five year term merely because this number has been used in the past or because it is the average of some sample of legislatures from other countries. Our choice must be consistent with some overall idea about what it is we are trying to accomplish with legislative representation. To see what we mean, notice that if the only consideration in the creation of a two-chamber legislature is the desire to reach some geographic compromise, then we would be unable to explain why so many states, even small non-federal ones, abide by the same format. Britain's House of Lords may exist out of tradition, but what accounts for the upper chambers of Austria, France or Iceland?

In fact there are other considerations. First, imagine a country divided into some number of equally populous districts, each of which elects one representative to the legislature. If only one candidate is elected from each district, then a majority of voters in a majority of districts can control all legislation. Since 50 per cent of 50 per cent equals 25 per cent, as few as one-quarter of the population can, theoretically, control the legislature. Normally we would not expect such extreme events to occur. But the bias a one-chamber legislature allows can create significant tensions when, for example, agricultural interests predominate over industrial concerns despite an opposite population balance.

There are several ways to avoid such problems. One is to draw legislative districts that are homogeneous in terms of the character of the people within them. But this alternative is impractical when populations are mixed. More importantly, it is divisive because, in drawing district boundaries, it explicitly pits different parts of society against each other in the struggle for initial advantage in the political process. Another alternative is to elect legislators using nation-wide proportional representation (PR). But PR entails its own types of cost. First, it increases the incentives for a fractured party system, which is something that states such as Russia and Ukraine ought to avoid. Second, it opens the door to the formation of purely ethnic or regional parties that may be unable to compromise their positions for fear of losing electoral support.

The third possibility is the two-chamber legislature, which accomplishes our purpose by requiring that legislation secure two majorities, one in each chamber. Indeed it is at this point that we encounter the logic of several other alternative constitutional provisions. Notice that two chambers has the intended effect of making it more difficult for a minority to control the legislature only to the extent that their bases of representation differ: otherwise the same voters can control both chambers. Thus effective implementation of the two-chamber legislative design requires that we avoid electing members of one chamber from precisely the same districts that we elect the members of the other.

This guideline can be met in any number of ways. In the United States, representatives from the lower chamber are elected from narrowly drawn constituencies and members of the Senate are elected by states. Members of the Senate in Canada are elected by province, whereas members of the lower chamber are elected by party-list PR. Germany and Russia mix these systems: members of the lower chamber are elected in both single-member districts and by national party-list PR, whereas members of the upper chamber represent federal subjects as in Canada and the USA.

To illustrate the protection a two-chamber legislature can provide minorities, consider the following example with nine voters. Suppose each voter is either of type X or of type Y (for example, ethnic group X or ethnic group Y), and suppose they live as shown in the representation below:

X   X   Y

Y   X   Y

X   Y   Y

Thus there are four X-type voters and five Y types, so that if each of these voters is allowed to be represented by a deputy in one chamber of the legislature, that chamber will contain a majority of Y types. Now suppose we create a second chamber by creating three horizontal election districts, each with three voters (that is, each line in the example is a district). Hence X-types are a majority in the first district, and Y types are a majority in the second and third districts. We can therefore reasonably suppose that Y-type deputies will be elected in the second and third districts. Thus not only will Y types dominate the first chamber, they will dominate the second as well, which may cause X-type voters to believe that their rights will not be respected by such a legislature. However, suppose instead that we create a second legislative chamber with three voters in each district as before, but with districts drawn vertically. In this variant the first two districts will most likely elect an X-type deputy since X types are a majority there, whereas only the third will elect a Y type. Thus while we can easily create a chamber in which Y types are a majority, we can also create a legislative chamber in which X types are in control. If we now require that legislation receive majority approval in both chambers, it must be the case that laws appeal to both X and Y types, or at least that sufficient compromises be made so that some X- and Y-type legislators can vote alike. Thus by the simple expedient of creating two chambers and drawing district boundaries carefully, we can promote compromise and minimize the chances that a majority can injure some minority.

But while this precaution may protect some minorities against majority tyranny, it should be evident that our example only illustrates a very sweeping type of control – one that is unlikely to operate effectively if public passions are aroused against very small minorities – those which cannot be a majority in either part of the legislature. As an additional precaution, then, we can elect members of the lower and upper houses to terms of different lengths. Although it may seem reasonable to want to make the government more responsive to public opinion by electing everyone at the same time, doing so leaves the state vulnerable to transitory public passions. Distinct terms of office in which we elect members of the lower house, say, every three years and one half of the members of the upper house every three years for six year terms provides some insurance against this possibility and lends greater stability and continuity to the government. A longer term for the upper chamber also induces its members to look at policy differently than members of the lower chamber: because they confront less immediate electoral imperatives, deputies to the upper chamber can take a longer-term view of things, which once again changes the hurdles any bill must jump over before it becomes law.

There are a great many other issues that must be addressed in designing a legislature. For example, we must decide:

- who should ratify treaties (usually the upper chamber, which generally represents regions of a federation or which may be elected to a longer term than the lower chamber);
- who should approve ministerial and court appointments (usually the upper chamber in presidential systems, the lower chamber in parliamentary ones);
- who should declare war (usually both chambers);
- who should authorize or void a declaration of emergency (usually both chambers);

- who must approve of constitutional amendments (usually both chambers plus citizens, directly or through their regional representatives, since they are of central importance to everyone and need to be given especially careful consideration);
- who, if anyone, can dismiss ministers (usually the lower chamber in parliamentary systems since it is that chamber which, being larger, is thought to be 'closer to the people').

A two-chamber legislature creates a good deal of flexibility in the ultimate design of a government. But regardless of the specifics of that design, it is important to understand that two chambers need not be viewed merely as a way to slow the processes of government or as a source of confusion and stalemate. A two-chamber design allows us to choose different electoral methods and different bases of representation so that the different parts of society each feel adequately represented and protected, thereby giving the government legitimacy and stability.

15. Parliaments and Presidents: Legislative Incoherence versus Authoritarian Rule?

Although the successor states of the USSR each provides for the office of the presidency in some form, there are those in every country who want to move things more in the direction of parliamentary government and others who want to strengthen the powers of the president. A parliamentary form, championed usually by leaders of a sitting legislature, has the advantage, it is argued, of avoiding the legislative–executive stalemate that characterized the conflict between Boris Yeltsin and the old People's Congress. A presidential system, on the other hand, is credited with being more in keeping with traditions of strong leadership that, armed with the power to issue decrees and to dismiss a recalcitrant legislature, seems essential in a period of massive economic dislocation.

The debate over alternatives usually is little more than a power struggle among political élites and it is anything but obvious that average citizens should care much about who wins and loses this debate. The issues, however, are important, if only because understanding the difference between parliamentary and presidential government helps people to understand how their government, regardless of form and regardless of whether the debate is an active one, works.

Looking first at parliamentary systems, their key feature is that the government serves at the legislature's discretion – or, more precisely, at the discretion of a majority in the legislature. As long as the government can command a majority of votes in parliament, it survives. But if a majority cannot be sustained, the government resigns or the president or prime minister calls for new legislative elections. Although we can imagine a number of variations, a president plays a minor role and, by making the executive a part of the legislature, executive–legislative conflict is minimized. By thus avoiding conflict between the government and the legislature, the argument goes, countries can better pursue a rational policy of economic reform. The national government speaks with a single voice – the voice of the parliamentary majority – through the person of the prime minister. However, parliamentary systems have two potential drawbacks. First:

- if parties in a parliamentary system are highly fractionalized, then legislative coalitions, and thus governments, are likely to be unstable.

This instability, common in systems without established party structures, can be as threatening to rational economic planning as executive–legislative deadlock. The second drawback is:

- because a government is elected by parliament, and because citizens only vote for members of the parliament, citizens have only indirect control over state policy in a parliamentary system.

Although indirect control is, by itself, not a bad thing, in parliamentary systems there is nothing to preclude parties that suffer losses at the polls from participating nevertheless in a government. Thus parliamentary government can, at least for a time, act contrary to public preferences and the vote.

Thus the performance of a parliamentary system depends on the character of its political parties. That character, in turn, depends on whether and how we satisfy another demand that arises frequently: the demand for proportional legislative representation (PR). Fearing that they will be under-represented if legislators are elected in single-member constituencies and realizing that legislative representation is the primary way to influence a government, ethnic minorities, occupational interests and religious groups will each demand some guarantee of representation. PR is the usual route to that end.

A common way to implement PR is for parties to submit candidate lists, for voters to vote for a preferred party, and for parties to win parliamentary seats in proportion to their support. A country can be divided into any number of multi-member districts or, as in Russia, Hungary, Germany and Israel, it can elect some or all deputies in one national constituency. Since any party that secures enough votes to overcome some explicit or implicit threshold (say, 5 per cent) wins seats, parties will seek to represent specific ideological, ethnic, social or religious cleavages, where the actual number of parties depends on the number and salience of those cleavages and the details of electoral procedures (such as the actual size of districts and minimum vote requirements).

PR seems an attractive addition to any government, parliamentary or otherwise, since it promises groups explicit representation. Even if representation is merely symbolic, symbolism can go a long way towards generating a sense that the state is legitimate. But PR has disadvantages. First:

- PR increases the incentives for politicians to engineer cleavages or to increase the salience of pre-existing ones, as when someone wants to advance their position by forming and leading a new party.

Thus PR gives extremists an audience and a potential role in the formation of a government. Second:

- although the process of forming a government offers some incentive for compromise, this incentive is attenuated by PR to the extent that parties must differentiate themselves to maintain electoral support. Moreover, society's conflicting demands are unlikely to be negotiated within party structures since a party must maintain a clear focus lest it find itself prey to those parties that provide such a focus.

These problems need not be consequential in a homogeneous society, but they can undermine the stability of countries such as Romania or Ukraine, which require less, not more, fragmented parties and less, not more, reasons for increasing the salience of ethnic–geographic disputes. PR alone, however, does not determine the nature of parties. We must also look at whether the presidency is a meaningful office. We turn, then, to the opposite of parliamentary government, presidential government, which is characterized by a chief of state who is directly elected for a fixed term and who heads a government he appoints (with the 'consent of the legislature') and that only he can dismiss. The presumed advantages of this model are:

- a directly elected president provides a focus for its aspirations and sense of nationhood, and offers a clear point of leadership in emergencies;

- governments are likely to be stable since they serve at the president's discretion, whose term is fixed;
- an independently elected and meaningful office of the presidency allows for the full implementation of the idea of a separation of powers.

A separation of powers was one of the touchstones of the Framers of the US constitution: 'The accumulation of all powers, legislative, executive, and judiciary, in the same hands, whether of one, a few, or many, and whether hereditary, self-appointed, or elected, may justly be pronounced the very definition of tyranny' (Madison, *Federalist Papers*, no. 47). Nevertheless, this last 'advantage' of presidentialism is seen by some as a disadvantage. Separate election and powers open the door, so the argument goes, to legislative–executive conflict, which may be especially severe if the president's party is not the one that controls the legislature. Later we argue that this problem has less to do with the general character of presidential systems and more with methods of election, but we cannot deny that the choice of parliamentary versus presidential system is often a choice between an efficient unitary state with the potential for instability versus rancorous bargaining between the legislature and the president.

Presidential systems are said also to have the drawback of presenting voters with an all-or-nothing choice – one side wins, all others lose. Parliamentary systems, the argument goes, allow all sides to 'win' something: legislative representation. But even if a party wins representation in parliament, it needn't participate in the government, and even if some groups are not explicitly represented in a president's administration, their interests may still be attended to by candidates who seek to form a majority in order to win the presidency.

Another drawback is that there may not be a 'best' way to elect presidents. A direct vote seems the simplest and most 'democratic' alternative, but there are many ways to implement this idea. One way is to require that a victorious candidate receive a majority of votes and to allow a run-off between the strongest candidates if no one receives a majority on the first ballot. This method seeks to ensure against the election of a candidate who receives, say, 30 per cent of the vote and who cannot claim a mandate to lead. But like PR, this scheme allows minor parties to block a first-ballot victory so they can negotiate their support between ballots, and thereby eliminates one of the advantages of presidentialism: the incentive of parties to coalesce and to negotiate conflict internally. A direct vote's problems are compounded by the requirement, common in the successor states of the Soviet Union, that turnout exceeds 50 per cent. However, it is a fallacy to believe that low turnout is 'bad' and high turnout is 'good'. Voters may abstain because they are dissatisfied and repulsed by all alternatives; but they may also abstain because all viable candidates are acceptable. Regardless of its source, a formal turnout requirement can only allow extremists to call for election boycotts without requiring that they formulate explicit policy alternatives. Some defects of a direct vote can be corrected if the minimum turnout requirement is deleted and if, instead of a majority, we require that the winning candidate receive some lesser percentage of the vote (say 40 per cent) before requiring a run-off. But now consider the problem of ensuring against a 'regional president' who secures most of his support from one geographic region and whose election is strongly opposed by voters in all other regions. One alternative is to eschew a single president and, as in Switzerland, to select a president on a rotating basis from representatives of its larger cantons. But as Simon Bolivar argued over a century and a half ago (*The Angostura Address*), such a system lacks, 'unity, continuity, and individual responsibility' and undermines most of the advantages of presidentialism. Nigeria earlier took a different approach by requiring that presidents secure at least 25 per cent of the votes in each of its federal subjects. Czechoslovakia, prior to its dissolution, required a majority in both its Czech and Slovak halves. Such devices, however, can yield contentious bargaining whenever no one meets these requirements, and they too allow regional parties to block anyone's election.

As with parliamentary government, then, the problems of presidentialism have less to do with any one characteristic of the system and more to do with the combination of factors. This fact is perhaps best illustrated by noting an especially dangerous combination: a directly elected president and a parliament elected by PR. Here we need to note simply that the powers of effective presidents derive less from their formal constitutional authority than they do from the fact that, as a nationally elected figure, a president is in a position to draw people's attention to critical issues, to mobilize support for specific policies and to propose compromises among contentious groups. The mere device of direct election gives a president a mandate to lead, and it is this mandate, more than any formal power, that presidents must learn to use in order to be effective. Indeed:

Rule 45: If we make the office of president constitutionally powerful, we only create incentives for the other parts of government to resist those powers.

Moreover, if parliament is elected by PR, the leaders of the larger parties there can also claim the same national mandate, which exacerbates conflict between president and parliament. In contrast, electing deputies by single-mandate districts leads them to focus on local issues and gives the president greater flexibility to negotiate compromises. Thus:

Rule 46: With a presidential system, we should avoid structures that permit legislators or legislative parties to claim the same national mandate that we would rightfully reserve for the president.

In general, then, there is no singularly and obviously 'best' way to implement democracy, and debates over the system most appropriate for a country need to appreciate the fact that the character of a political system is determined not by any single factor, such as the relative power of the president versus the legislature. It is a function also of electoral procedures and the types of party that emerge to compete for public office. Moreover, no system is perfect and no system offers a guarantee of stability. PR promises minorities a formal voice; but it can result in a highly fractionalized party structure incapable of achieving compromise on divisive issues. A direct vote for president allows voters to pass direct judgement on a government's performance, but it need not preclude the possibility of parties that form merely to block one or another candidate from securing a mandate to lead. None of these difficulties, however, is an argument for not making any choice. People and political systems will adapt to different constitutions, and it is more important to choose *some* system and *some* constitution rather than search for a non-existent perfection.

16. Emergency Clauses: Essential Precautions or A Lack of Faith?

Few people question that most of the successor states of the Soviet Union are in crisis. Unsurprisingly, many point to mainland China or to Taiwan as models usefully combining authoritarian control and the development of a market economy. Others say to hell with markets or transitions to democracy; dictatorship and central planning wasn't so bad after all. Our sympathies obviously lie with democracy. But rather than merely expressing sympathies, our intent in this chapter is to examine the advisability of constitutional emergency clauses designed to deal with crises of different types. One reason for this focus is that such clauses seem a reasonable compromise between the desire to be democratic and the pragmatic requirement of strong leadership during a period of unsettling transition. Thus some constitutions direct the legislature to pass laws that grant special powers to a chief of state in an emergency; others offer elaborate provisions that identify who can declare an emergency, who must ratify such a declaration, the circumstances that qualify as emergencies, the duration of a state of emergency, and the procedures whereby an emergency regime is ended. Regardless of the details of how this compromise is attempted, we argue here that not only is no such compromise possible, but also that it is unnecessary.

The most evident problem with emergency clauses is their potential for abuse. Indeed it takes a good many fingers and a good many hands to count those 'democracies' that have been transformed into something else under the cover of a declared emergency. Our purpose here, however, is to make a different argument. In broad outline, the logical parts of this argument are as follows:

1. Avoiding any abuse of power in the event that an emergency regime is imposed requires that government function with some internal checks and balances.

2. The power of those authorized to declare a state of emergency must be controlled by the other parts of government, lest power be usurped.

3. If we can restrain the abuse of power in an emergency, then no such clauses are required.

Thus to state our argument as an additional rule of democratic institutional design:

> *Rule 47*: If a normally functioning state cannot accommodate emergencies, then the aggregation of power in a few hands will threaten democracy regardless of the controls a constitution tries to establish.

The opportunities for an abuse of power arise, of course, from the fact that a declaration of emergency allows the state or specific office holders in it to do unusual things, such as delay or otherwise cancel elections, incarcerate persons indefinitely or abrogate specified (and even some unspecified) rights. Each such action threatens a dangerous precedent, and any reasonable proposal for a constitutional emergency clause tries to ensure the existence of checks on emergency powers that can be applied by the legislature, regional governments or the courts. But such checks on abuse operate only if, aside from the special circumstances of the emergency, the state otherwise functions normally. This fact, which we discuss in more detail shortly, should be kept in mind as we examine the situations that an emergency clause seeks to treat.

Briefly, the situations commonly identified by different constitutions as an emergency include attempts to overthrow the constitutional system, large-scale economic dislocation, mass unrest, inter-ethnic conflict, natural disasters, epidemics and epizootic diseases, external aggression, threats to the people's safety and a general incapacity of the state to meet its obligations. This list yields four general categories of emergency: natural disasters, economic disintegration, external threats and internal threats. Of these four categories, only the second and fourth seem to require any special attention. The first, natural disasters, unless of unprecedented magnitude, are likely to be localized events and of no threat to the normal operation of the state. What special or unusual powers does the state require to treat floods or epidemics? If such events cannot be anticipated and provided for by normal legislation and treated with some measure of consensus, then no constitution, regardless of form, is viable. The third possibility, invasion, threatens not only the state but the nation and, as with natural disasters, it is difficult to imagine a society that cannot act to meet such calamities or that cannot reach a consensus on appropriate procedures, even 'extra-constitutional' ones. This type of emergency is perhaps the least am-biguous and is the one most easily treated in that part of the constitu-tion that enumerates the powers of the legislature – for example, by including the clause, '[the legislature] shall make provision for the functioning of the state in the event that a state of war exists between _____ and any other foreign power'.

Looking more closely at the reasons for supposing that a normally functioning state can be expected to handle invasions and floods, we should of course recognize that states may be required from time to time to do unusual things with respect to, say, civil liberties. People may have to be quarantined, barred from entering territory, moved without immedi-ate compensation or prohibited from revealing military preparations. But our willingness to turn such matters over to 'the authorities' – to the military, the police and the courts – and to allow them some freedom of action, requires the existence of internal checks. If the legislature and the courts can oversee and regulate these authorities, if a chief of state and the legislature can ensure that the courts are impartial, and if the courts and the president can focus public attention on the legislature to ensure that its actions are timely and constitutional, then a consensus on appro-priate responses to an emergency is likely to emerge.

Democracies, then, allow various parts of the government temporar-ily to assume special powers to the extent that people are certain that they can be restrained from overstepping the bounds of reasonable action. And, most importantly, the thing that acts as the constraint on action is the *normal* system of internal checks and balances that a well-designed constitution establishes. In this way:

> *Rule 48*: A constitutional democracy is something other than a system of inflexible rules that require special provisions to handle every unusual circumstance and to treat every crisis. No one has yet discovered the trick to writing such rules, and indeed there are probably theorems in mathemat-ics that tell us that such rules cannot exist. Instead we rely on a 'balance of powers' within the state, where the interests of the state's component parts are formed by each part's different connection to those the state is supposed to serve, the people.

Of course, if there is a test of this 'theory of democratic government', it lies in the area of the second and fourth categories of emergency:

economic turmoil and domestic insurrection. These circumstances appear to be a different species of animal, requiring separate treatment in a constitution. So let us consider them, beginning with insurrection.

Presumably, this type of emergency concerns an attempted secession by, say, one of Russia's republics, by the Crimea from Ukraine, or simply armed ethnic conflict and any of the parts of the ex-Soviet Union. Such emergencies may initially be confined to a small region but, as Britain's experience with Northern Ireland illustrates, they can be exported to endanger everyone. And whether localized or exported, such conflicts are often accompanied by the wholesale breakdown of law and order and, in the most extreme cases, by the takeover of a region by undemocratic forces. In this event, we cannot rely on regional authorities to resolve matters or to call for timely intervention by the national government.

Because unilateral action by a national government, without the constitutional authority that an emergency provision might offer, appears to violate federal principles, a true 'constitutional emergency' seems inescapable. Nevertheless, the granting of special authority to a chief of state or prime minister through the normal actions of the legislature should be adequate to treat this type of emergency. If a constitution guarantees a democratic government to all parts of a country, then the national government can justify intervention on the basis of an appeal to a part of the constitution that does not explicitly refer to emergencies. Moreover, the protection afforded a federation's constituent parts against unwarranted actions and unreasonable interpretations of 'democratic government' is the normally functioning national government itself, as a consequence of the fact that the legislature, in addition to representing people, also represents the federation's parts.

Turning, then, to our last category of emergencies – economic ones that are today most closely associated with the transition from a planned to a market economy – this is, of course, the arena that affords us an almost daily view of the inability of the state to formulate policies that are coherent, consistent and timely. With so much effort devoted to political manoeuvre and conflict, and with an unregulated self-interest appearing to drive economies to ruin, 'strong leadership' seems the only course: 'Give _____ [you fill in the blank] the authority to reshape the economy, our political and judicial system, and our system (or non-system) of property rights'. What choice do we have, some people can ask, but to take a temporary step back from the incoherence of democratic process when all that process can yield is chaos in the short term?

But what reasons do people have for supposing that such chaos is endemic to Russia, Ukraine, Armenia or wherever? Do we have some large sample of democratic experiments in these countries that all resulted in the same thing? Should we plan the transition to democracy on the assumption that chaos will persist into the indefinite future? Indeed are we certain that any apparent chaos is not without beneficial consequences, including the gradual accumulation of capital in the hands of those most likely to reinvest it productively in the future? Despite assertions to the contrary, no one knows with certainty what policies will move a country to prosperity with the least pain. There are no economic messiahs, no 'quick fixes' and no paths to progress that only a few can see. If no one knows what's best or if they know it only accidentally, what is the advantage of authoritarian rule, however temporary? How can we be certain that our choice of 'temporary dictator' *is* the person who knows best? The best we can hope for is that people will press their arguments upon each other, and that out of this debate, however incoherent, will come compromises, experiments (both successful and unsuccessful) and, hopefully, a few new ideas.

It appears, then, that we must reject any possibility of a constitutional accommodation of emergencies. We have rejected authoritarian rule, however authorized, and we have also argued that contentious debate, which implementation of emergency provisions can foreclose, can yield a clearer view of alternatives. Is there, then, any proper role for some form of constitutional emergency clause?

In fact there is a role: the *coordination* of the state. The problem with economic emergencies is that there are numerous competing alternative policies, each vying for the title 'best'. And because each of them gives special advantage to someone, it is difficult to use the ordinary processes of government to select one of them. Owing to disagreements within it, the legislature may be unable to organize itself appropriately, or the legislature and president, although appreciating the need for timely action, may be unable to agree on, or otherwise choose, some course of action aside from doing nothing. And although no one policy may be best, the selection of any one of them may be better than incoherence and no policy at all. In fact we suspect that it is here that we find the argument against what we have said thus far. Specifically, emergency clauses are not designed to choose 'the best' policy; they are designed instead to ensure that *some* policy, however imperfect, is adopted.

However, rather than conclude that advocates of constitutional emergency provisions are correct, viewing crises this way tells us how to fashion provisions that avoid excessive concentrations of power, but that give some part of government the ability to coordinate or to initiate those actions that will lead the different parts of the state to concerted action. For example, instead of granting a president the power of decrees, suppose we give him the right to call the legislature into special session and to require that it consider only the temporary emergency legislation he proposes. The special power of the president in this instance is the authority to focus public debate and to set the legislative agenda: to require that his proposals take precedence in legislative deliberations. There cannot be any usurpation of power since the legislature can continue to negotiate with the president over details. And since the state continues to function normally, there is no need to abrogate rights or at least to abrogate them in a way that sets dangerous precedents.

It may be hard to convince readers that so weak a provision can accomplish much of anything, especially in light of the economic distress that some states confront. Indeed what we propose leads to a process that is not much different from what occurred throughout most of 1992 in Russia. Although sometimes chaotic, and despite the events that unfolded in September and October of 1993, we should also keep in mind that throughout most of this period compromises were reached and no one was suddenly given a free but unwanted tour of Siberia. The eventual dissolution of the People's Congress had more to do with Yeltsin's failure to understand the mechanics of democracy – with the need to consult and cajole members of the Congress to bring them over to his side – than anything else. The new legislature does not function better today because it contains fresh faces, because deputies live in fear of tanks or because special emergency provisions direct events. It works instead because normal democratic process – the fear of elections and the promise of winning higher office – is now more salient to those who hold the reigns of power. Those who fear that normal democratic process can only lead to further chaos and eventual dictatorship should keep in mind that stronger emergency provisions in the constitutions of other countries are more often than not the source of emergencies and not their solution. Put simply:

> *Rule 49*: The most effective 'emergency clause' is a well-written constitution that establishes a viable balance of power among the different parts of the state, that gives those parts a clear connection to the people, and that gives political leaders an incentive to prepare beforehand for emergencies and to resolve them in an effective and timely manner when they arise.

Before we conclude this discussion of emergencies, there is one last issue that needs to be addressed: the widespread crime and corruption that seems an inescapable part of the transition from communism to democracy and free enterprise. News reports from Moscow, for example, amply reveal the extent of the problem, which is particularly damaging to democracy whenever it permeates official institutions – a circumstance that appears to describe Russian politics today as well as the politics of the other successor states of the Soviet Union. The temptation, then, is to combat the problem by suspending constitutional rights – especially those pertaining to due process of law – and to give special authority to various internal security agencies. This is the route presently being taken by Moscow authorities under the sanction of President Yeltsin.

We can appreciate the concern that crime occasions, especially violent crime (as when legislators and judges themselves are threatened or even killed), and the sympathy for special measures that is likely to be felt by the population generally. But even if corruption and crime permeate official institutions, there is little reason to disallow the judicial system from exercising oversight over whatever special measures are taken and whatever special authority is granted to internal security agencies. The dangers are especially great in presidential systems, since moving such authority to the office of the president or to some ministry under his control merely allows a dangerous concentration of power within one branch of the state, and forecloses the opportunity for the remaining branches – especially the judiciary – to act as a safeguard against abuse. And we can be certain that abuses will occur. The suspension of constitutional rights in the name of public safety is a dangerous act not merely because of the abuses it allows, but also because wresting back such authority is more often than not an impossible undertaking. Those with such authority normally have every incentive to resist a diminution of their power – a power that cannot be checked by any other branch of the government.

None of this is to say, of course, that the judicial branch is immune to corruption any more than any other part of the state. Nevertheless, every effort should be made to combat crime and corruption using 'normal' procedures until there is compelling evidence that one part of the state or another is incapable of functioning owing to the corruption that permeates it. Indeed even in states in which corruption seems a part of political tradition (Italy, Columbia?), members of the judiciary, often at great personal risk and sacrifice, have performed their duty.

Until and unless there is some consensus that this branch of government cannot function to provide oversight against abuses of constitutional rights, citizens in a democracy are well advised to resist the excuses offered by one part of government or the other to short-circuit constitutional limitations on their authority.

17. Russia's Choices: An Accident Waiting to Happen?

Reform has two dimensions – an economic one and a political one – and although lip-service is paid generally to the proposition that these two dimensions are fused and that one cannot be attacked without attacking the other, they are too frequently approached, especially on the territory of the former Soviet Union, as though different principles guide each. In fact the same basic principle ought to direct our confrontation of both.

The economic reformer's strategies are stated in terms of laws on private property, banking and contracts, and take the form of government policies on tariffs, taxes, privatization, borrowing and subsidies. Regardless of the school of thought to which a reformer adheres, it is understood that these laws and policies need to be manipulated in accordance with a common principle: socially desirable outcomes cannot be willed or wished into existence; they derive, if at all, from the ways in which government action and economic institutions channel individual self-interest. People cannot be made to work, save, invest or invent through mere oratory: people must be given the incentives to do these things in natural and self-sustaining ways. Thus by manipulating government policies and by nurturing the development of appropriate economic institutions, reform must make working, saving, investing and inventing in people's immediate self-interest.

Although how best to apply the principle of self-interest in economics is imperfectly understood, its applicability with respect to the second dimension of reform, the political one, is even less well appreciated. But appreciated or not:

Rule 50: The transition to democracy consists of the design and manipulation of institutions – of schemes of legislative representation, election laws and constitutional allocations of power – that render certain actions and the pursuit of certain outcomes in people's self-interest.

Circumstances differed greatly from those that characterize any ex-communist state, but the parallelism of economic and political reform was well understood by the framers of the US constitution. For example, when debating the method whereby judges ought to be selected, Benjamin Franklin sought to inspire a fuller consideration of the alternatives among delegates to the Philadelphia Convention by relating a Scottish method 'in which the nomination proceeded from the lawyers, who always selected the ablest of the profession in order to get rid of him and share his practice among themselves' (James Madison, *Notes on The Constitutional Convention*). Applied to the protections democracy provides against tyranny, James Madison generalized Franklin's example when he wrote: 'The great security against the gradual concentration of the several powers in the same department consists in giving to those who administer each department the necessary constitutional means and *the personal motives* to resist encroachments of the others…Ambition must be made to counter ambition' (*Federalist*, no. 51, emphasis added).

It is this principle that decision-makers elsewhere have not yet applied with consistency in their approach to political reform. Political reform is too often viewed through the old lens of command and control. Rather than pay heed to the complex and often imperfectly understood ways in which democratic institutions shape incentives and sustain themselves, it is only the outer shells of institutions that are manipulated. And with people's perceptions of the future obscured by the uncertainties of transition, and with those in power sharing an understandable reluctance to relinquish their authority, those manipulations are motivated less by a search for a stable democratic order than they are by the quest for immediate political advantage.

Even though it is arguably further along the road to reform than any other successor state of the USSR (except possibly the Baltic states), the problems here are best illustrated by Russia. The lament that politics there is merely a war of personalities may be an apt summary of the current situation. But describing the situation thus and searching for a cadre of new, more enlightened leaders can only yield disappointment. If the principle of self-interest is valid, then the actions of any new cadre will be dictated by the same incentives that guide the actions of the current ones.

Meaningful political reform requires that we look to those things that shape incentives, especially of those who control the coercive reins of government, and it is the failure to do these things carefully that now bedevils Russia's transition to democracy. Three things in particular confound the development of a stable democracy there:

1. The way in which the new Russian constitution shapes presidential–legislative relations.
2. The general approach to federalism and the way in which Moscow tries to meet the demands for regional autonomy.
3. The failure to understand the determinants of political parties, the role of parties in resolving conflict, and the relationship between parties and the variegated interests that characterize a market economy.

It might seem that each of these things can be treated separately: amend the constitution to reduce the powers of the presidency; negotiate new relationships between federal subjects and Moscow; and reform campaign finance laws. But such a view ignores how the incentives of *all* political élites are determined by their relationship to the ultimate sovereign in a democracy, and how these incentives interact to influence each other and all other things simultaneously. Our argument, then, is that piecemeal reform or the signing of Civic Accords will not resolve the problems of Russian democracy. Instead we need to look at the fundamental institutional determinants of incentives. Otherwise we can predict that:

- the president and factions within parliament will continue to claim a national mandate to lead, and all constitutional points of conflict between president and parliament will be active ones;
- the struggle between decision-makers in Moscow and regional élites will continue unabated;
- parties will remain highly fragmented, parliamentary elections will serve largely as primaries in the quest for the main prize of the presidency, and successful parties will be those that best frame nationalistic and authoritarian appeals.

PRESIDENTIAL–PARLIAMENTARY RELATIONS

Looking first at the relationship of the president to parliament, the new Russian constitution, ratified by popular referendum in 1993, gives every indication of extending the conflict between these two branches of government that precipitated Yeltsin's coup against the old parliament. Parliament legislates but the president can make law (by decree insofar as the law is silent). The president can veto acts of parliament, but the parliament can veto decrees (by passing contrary laws and by overriding presidential vetoes of those laws). Furthermore, the president can hire and fire ministers, but parliament can vote no confidence and compel the president to choose between replacing his ministers and scheduling new parliamentary elections. The constitution, then, adheres only to a superficial notion of a separation of powers and, aside from those special powers that give the president the upper hand in disputes (to dismiss parliament, to call referenda, to suspend local acts and laws, and to interpret the constitution as the 'protector of the constitution'), it places the president and parliament in direct opposition to each other.

In a state with strong democratic traditions, such institutional entanglements might compel compromise. But the likelihood of compromise depends not only on necessity, but also on incentives. The likelihood that Russia will choose the compromises that characterize stable democracies versus the conflicts that characterize an unstable one depends on whether political élites find it in their self-interest to engage in compromise rather than conflict.

In tracing the incentives of a president and parliamentary deputies, it is reasonable to begin with the assumption that, patriotic or venal, political élites seek power. But how power is secured and applied depends on the relationship between élites and those who directly or indirectly confirm their position: the people. It is this relationship that determines the fates of those who fill public office in a democracy, and it is this relationship that determines the private consequences of compromise or of the failure to compromise. Unfortunately, the details of the relationship in Russia between public officeholders and the people, as established by law, decree or constitutional provision, undermine the prospects for compromise and democratic stability.

Although the rules for presidential selection are not yet firmly established, it is almost certain that the next Russian president will be directly elected using the simple 'majority with run-off' procedure described earlier. We have no quarrel with direct elections. However, if Yeltsin could successfully claim a national mandate on the basis of the questionable 1993 referendum, then a new president, directly elected and guaranteed a majority vote on the first or second ballot, will claim the same mandate on an even firmer footing.

Mandates are valuable things for anyone choosing to exert leadership and it is imperative that, given his constitutional powers, a president possess a mandate to lead. But the problem here is the combination of direct election of the president with the electoral system used for the Duma elections. The current procedure for electing deputies there – half in single-member constituencies and half by national party-list proportional representation (PR) – was implemented to facilitate the formation of national parties and to ensure against the election of those opponents of reform that could marshall strong local electoral support. What was less well appreciated, however, was the fact that with candidates for the Duma competing through national party lists and with parliamentary elections occurring before, and independently of, the presidential contest, any majority coalition in the Duma can assert the same mandate claimed by the president – a mandate that Zhirinovsky claimed with only 23 per cent of the vote in 1993 and which someone with any larger percentage is certain to assert is his. Thus with both the president and parliament claiming the same thing – a mandate to lead – and with the new constitution confusing the issue of 'who is in charge', the stage is set for conflict and crisis of precisely the same sort that characterized the early stages of Russian democracy.

FEDERAL RELATIONS

A second manifestation of the failure to understand the role of incentives in political reform is the way Moscow tried to form its relations with subjects of the Federation. Aside from the conflict between the president and the Congress that characterized the first years of Russian democracy, no issue was more salient than that of federalism, especially the position of Russia's ethnic republics. Who was to control Russia's vast resources and who was to oversee privatization of state property? Were the republics sovereign? Could they conduct their own foreign policy and could they secede from the Federation? What power did Moscow have over regional Soviets? Whose laws were supreme? Should Russia's federalism be symmetric or should the ethnic republics, which historically enjoyed greater autonomy than the other regions, be treated differently than those other parts?

Rather than discuss the federal form a state should choose, here we want only to make three observations about the constitutional bargain that was ultimately established in Russia and the negotiations that preceded it. The first observation is that formal negotiations over this relationship focused on a Federal Treaty that enumerated the jurisdictions belonging exclusively to Moscow and jurisdictions shared by Moscow and the republic. Second, republics demanded that they be identified as 'sovereign states', with the presumption that this label, combined with the terms of the Federal Treaty, would protect their autonomy. Third, republics demanded the authority to renegotiate bilaterally the details of their relationships with Moscow, so that separate deals could be struck.

These facts give rise to several questions about whether an understanding of incentives played any role in the design of Russia's federal form. Was any mechanism envisioned for enforcing an agreement? Was any process identified for resolving the ambiguities inherent in a treaty that encompassed all activities and responsibilities of the state? What consequences were envisioned for the creation of a federation that treated republics differently than the predominantly Russian regions? Unfortunately, little attention was paid to the institutional determinants of incentives. With eyes focused on political expediency, Yeltsin's April 1993 draft constitution, offered when the resolution of his conflict with the Congress was in doubt, identified republics as sovereign entities, gave them the authority to negotiate their relationship with Moscow on a bilateral basis and, in a provision that could hardly be taken seriously, required that the republics' representation in the upper legislative chamber, the Federation Council, be increased to whatever extent necessary in order to ensure their control of it. All of these special provisions were dropped in the final version once Yeltsin no longer needed the republics in his struggle against the Congress.

The final version of the constitution adhered to the idea of enumerated powers, and incorporated the long lists of exclusive and joint jurisdictions that were the core of the Federal Treaty. Whatever protection the constitution provides for federal subjects is contained in the powers of the Federation Council. With two deputies selected from each of Russia's 89 regions, the Council approves any internal changes in borders, regulates the president's emergency powers, approves the use of troops and declarations of war, convicts the president following impeachment by the Duma, and approves presidential nominations to the Constitutional Court. Two constitutional provisions, however, weaken the Council's powers. First, the Duma can override (with a two-thirds vote) the Council's rejection of any law. The second provision is a vaguely worded requirement that the Council be 'formed' from the executive and legislative branches of federal subjects. Although compatible with the idea that the governor and chief legislative officer of each region should be deputies to the Federation Council, the president can use his decree authority to establish any method of selection he prefers.

The undifferentiated treatment of republics and other regions suggests that Russia has opted for a symmetric federalism in which the autonomy of federal subjects is protected by the upper legislative chamber. But because of the failure to consider incentives, we find no such guarantee. Recall our earlier discussion of federalism and the indirect mechanisms whereby states in the USA ensure their autonomy against the powers of the national government. Recall in particular that the source of that protection lies in the requirement that individual states control the election of the members of both branches of Congress that represent them and their residents, which ensures that political parties in the USA are primarily state and local organizations. Although competition for the presidency dictates an equilibrium of two national coalitions, it is a decentralized party system that oversees the re-election of individual members of the legislature. With their political fortunes tied to local constituencies and party organizations, national legislators have an incentive, insofar as it matches the incentives of their constituencies, to resist the encroachments of national governmental power.

Insofar as what it is that maintains this arrangement as an equilibrium we need look no further than legislative self-interest – legislators have no incentive to change the rules of a game in which they are the winners. Thus protection of state and local autonomy is provided by the connection between legislators and constituents and the incentives this creates among legislators to represent their constituencies; this connection, in turn, is maintained by the unwillingness of legislators to change a game they are especially skilled to play. Unfortunately, no such equilibrium is promised for Russia. First, although the first session of the Federation Council was filled by direct plurality voting, that procedure was a temporary measure dictated by Yeltsin's dissolution of regional Supreme Soviets. It remains an open question as to whether popular election will again be used or whether some type of appointment process, directed by Moscow or regional governments, will be used. Second, Russia's election law establishes a Central Election Commission with broad authority to regulate election rules and procedures. Thus once this Commission begins to exert its authority, there is no guarantee that Russia's regions will play any significant role in determining the election process. Finally, electing half the Duma by party-list PR undermines any incentive for Duma deputies elected by a party list to represent, and be protective of, local and regional autonomy.

POLITICAL PARTIES

Turning finally to the character of political parties, a common lament, summarized by Yegor Gaidar's adviser, Vladimir Mau ('The "Ascent of the Inflationists', *Journal of Democracy*, April 1994), is that: 'Economic interest groups are now the key players in Russian politics; political parties, by contrast, have been and remain weak and unstable'. Similarly, displaying a complete failure to understand how and why parties form, Vladimir Shumieko, Speaker of the Federation Council, proposed postponement of parliamentary elections until a strong party system emerged. But if, as we have argued throughout this volume, parties exist to win elections and if their character is determined by the rules under which elections are held, then three characteristics of Russia's electoral institutions inhibit the formation of parties of the type Mau, Shumeko and others profess to want. These features are: (1) non-simultaneous presidential and parliamentary elections; (2) implementation of the majority run-off election procedure for presidential elections; and (3) the election of half the Duma by party-list PR.

These three features operate individually and together. The failure to require simultaneous elections not only denies a president the opportunity to carry a workable legislative majority with him into office, but discourages having a president play the key role in organizing a party. The majority run-off procedure discourages the withdrawal of otherwise uncompetitive parties who might block a first-ballot victor so they can negotiate their support in the run-off. And electing half the Duma by national party-list PR contributes to party fragmentation and undermines the incentive for parties to consolidate around non-radical candidates and platforms. And together these features produce a system whereby the parliamentary election stage acts much like America's presidential primary elections. It is here that presidential aspirants can try to demonstrate their attractiveness prior to the presidential election. However, unlike the American process, there is no stage (except the very last ballot) whereby presidential aspirants *qua* parties are eliminated. Instead parties are encouraged to 'hang in there', both by the prospect of parliamentary representation and by the possibility of success or influence in the presidential balloting.

REFORM

Nothing we have said implies the possibility of a quick fix for Russia's political ailments. But we can offer three suggestions that can move things in a proper direction. The first change is to abandon the use of a 'majority with run-off' in presidential elections. Following Costa Rica (whose stability stands out among Latin American states), a run-off should occur only if no one receives more than 40 per cent of the vote. Indeed:

> *Rule 51*: By lowering the threshold to 40 per cent in a direct-vote run-off system, we give weak candidates and parties a stronger incentive to refrain from running or even forming, and we in fact make it more likely that some candidate will secure a majority on the first ballot.

Put simply, we can make a majority winner more likely by simply not requiring it.

The second suggestion concerns the method of electing deputies to the Duma. One possible reform is to allow each federal subject to determine the method of election of its own parliamentary representatives. Abandoning prescription and regulation by Moscow in favour of decentralization strengthens Russia's federal structure, decreases incentives for party factionalism, and decreases the ability of parties within the legislature to claim a mandate that contravenes the president's. Alternatively, following the German model, deputies to the Duma can be elected by PR within each of, say, 10 or 15 election districts, which would decrease party factionalism and would facilitate the growth of regional party organizations, but which would nevertheless give parties a national focus. However, regardless of the specifics of reform here, nearly anything is better than the current arrangement, which is simply the world's largest experiment with national party-list PR, which dooms Russia to a muddled party system, with all of the incoherence of parliamentary process such a system implies, and which allows one or more parties in parliament to claim a mandate in opposition to the president.

Our third suggestion is to hold presidential and parliamentary elections simultaneously. When combined with our other suggestions, simultaneous election affords the president a better opportunity to do what is uncommon in ex-communist states: to exert leadership. Leadership, however vague and ill-defined, needs to be distinguished from simple political control. Throughout Russian history, those directing the state have relied on the most evident and extraordinary instruments of political power rather than on the democratic arts of persuasion, compromise and the power that originates from being seen as the spokesman of the people. The lament that Russia is at the mercy of powerful personalities contesting for the reins of power may be accurate. But simultaneity allows an escape from this dangerous equilibrium. Coupled with direct election is:

> *Rule 52*: Simultaneous presidential and parliamentary elections allow presidents to bargain away some of their formal constitutional authority and to look instead to an even more secure basis of power – the people's mandate.

Our suggestions cannot resolve all of what ails Russia. Those ailments are too complex and pervasive to yield to any simple, short-term corrective. However, unlike mere exhortations to 'behave better' or unfeasible demands that this or that provision of the constitution be changed or abolished, our suggestions can be implemented without running afoul of any pre-existing self-interest. But regardless of the steps that are ultimately taken, it is imperative that political reform proceeds in accordance with the principle of self-interest and with the understanding that the implications of reform cannot be ascertained without first tracing the incentives it creates or fails to create. This is the lesson that Russia's transition to democracy – successful or otherwise – ought to teach other states. Others will choose constitutional electoral arrangements that differ from Russia's. But different or otherwise, those arrangements must be chosen only after a careful examination is undertaken of the incentives they establish both individually and in combination with each other.

18.   Can We Be a Democracy?

The answer to the question that forms this chapter's title among people who must count their money daily to see if they have enough for a meal must be 'who cares – bring back the old days when we could at least afford whatever was available!'. And for others, especially if they follow politics closely, the only answer seems to be no. Other questions certainly look more relevant: will there be a coup? When will our anarchic politics require the intervention of a new authoritarian ruler? So accuse us of excessive optimism or unrealistic idealism, but *our* answer to this chapter's question, regardless of which part of the former Soviet Union we refer to, is yes! Our argument is that the politics of the Baltic states and of Central Europe will soon not look much different to those of Western Europe. Russia, Belarus and Ukraine are close to being democracies – messy ones, incomplete ones, unstable ones, ones in which fraud and corruption are the rule rather than the exception, and ones to which a goodly number of persons are only weakly committed – but they are very nearly democracies nevertheless. Pessimism rather than optimism seems warranted only for the states of the Caucasus and the remaining republics of the ex-USSR.

The assumption that few of these states are democratic or are about to become so rests in part on the belief that incoherent and inefficient political systems cannot be liberal democracies. Democracies – at least stable ones – are thought to be orderly things in which courts protect civil liberties, people vote on a regular basis, legislators deliberate, politicians abide by constitutional limits on their power, corruption is rare and policy-making proceeds according to well-defined procedures. Arguments over fundamental political structures, proposals to cancel the next election, shoving and pushing on the floor of the legislature, and ministers who contradict each other daily are things, it is assumed, that cannot be the elements of a stable democracy or of a democracy that promises to be stable in the future.

But the creation of a democratic state is rarely a simple process. The relationship between national and state governments in America is under continuous revision; Canada's future today hangs in the balance with the threat of secession by Quebec; Belgian unity strains under linguistic conflicts; and Italy in 40 years has had as many governments as America has had presidents in 200. It is true that most of the pieces of the ex-USSR do not possess many of the components of a normal democratic state: political parties with national organizations and comprehensive policy agendas, smoothly functioning courts, a well-defined system of property rights, an economic infrastructure that allows for rational economic planning, democratic local self-government, a professional legislature with a clear internal structure, a universal commitment to regularly scheduled elections, and the complex array of citizen interest groups that mobilize people in an orderly way to influence state policy. That these things do not exist in full measure, however, is no reason to predict that they cannot exist, albeit in primitive form. Governments may still rely too much on decrees to promulgate policy, they may continue to control the media and the press more than we prefer, and bribery and corruption may have become too pervasive and too readily accepted as a way to do business. But most citizens have made the commitment to constitutional democracy, and most public officials would prefer to advance their careers in accordance with constitutional principles, if only because that is the way to secure the approbation of other states.

It is true, of course, that the commitment to democratic process is not always made for reasons we might prefer. Yeltsin's strongest opponents, for example, may have moderated their criticism of his constitution not because they believe in democracy but rather because they see it as providing a route to securing the reins of power. Nor can we deny that government policies or pronouncements still vacillate between contradictions. But vacillation and contradiction only reflect the fact that no one knows the best course of economic reform. It is hard to believe that the same confusion and contentiousness would not characterize any democracy undergoing similar upheaval. And although we can detect the emergence of a commitment to individual rights, we would hardly argue that every public official shares this commitment or that everyone understands rights in the same way. We are certainly alarmed by decrees in Russia that violate constitutional rights in the name of social stability and the war against crime, just as we are concerned about the definitions of citizenship that have emerged in Estonia or Latvia. Nevertheless, people are increasingly free to express their views and judicial processes are gradually emerging whereby these rights and others can be protected. There is, in fact, as close an acceptance of these rights as we might expect to see in most democracies: a xenophobic Japan discriminates against its minorities; Western Europe struggles against fascist and Nazi nostalgia; and incidents of police violence directed at blacks in America have hardly disappeared from the news.

This is not to say that the job of political reconstruction in Central or Eastern Europe is done. No one believes that all that remains is to lead economies to recovery and to wait for democracy to develop on its own. Democracy's survival is not guaranteed. First, most of the states in question require new constitutions that give unambiguous guidance to the state's function, and even those states with new constitutions – Russia and Belarus, for example – merely possess transitional documents. Second, the sub-parts of the state – regional and local governments – require democratic constitutions or charters since, without them, democracy cannot flourish at any level. Third, ethnically heterogeneous states must develop federal forms and local governmental institutions that allow for a coherent pattern of regional autonomy. Fourth, states must construct election laws and procedures that make the competition for office coherent and responsive to citizen interests, and that at the same time minimize the possibilities of fraud. Finally, the people themselves must learn to stop looking for the 'right' leader; they must instead begin to place their faith in the political institutions they themselves create.

We need also to appreciate that being a new democracy is not the same thing as being a mature one. A new democracy should not be expected to produce the same things as one that has existed for 10 or 20 years. A baby has little control over what emerges from either of its ends, it cannot dress or feed itself, it operates largely by instinct, it relies on the paternalism of those around it for survival, and it can hardly explain or comprehend why all of this is so. It cannot move furniture, solve maths problems or raise a family. But these facts do not mean that a baby is not a person. We merely understand that to raise this person from childhood to adulthood requires having the right expectations about its capabilities at each stage of its development. So it is with democracies.

A two- or three-year-old democracy cannot produce instant guarantees of rights, well-ordered and smoothly functioning political institutions, coherent policy or even leaders who understand why things work as they do. It may seem difficult to answer questions such as, 'who needs this thing called democracy?' or, 'why don't we dispense with all this nonsense, and merely adopt a political system compatible with our traditions – autocracy or, minimally, a strong leader who can rule by decree?' in ways that accord with the recommendations of this volume. Nevertheless, we should be able to see now that the answers to these questions are contained in part in democracy's definition. People must have leaders because society must be coordinated to act, and democracy is merely a method whereby the people are empowered to choose their leaders and the directions of public policy in an orderly way that protects individual rights. All the rest – bicameral versus unicameral legislatures, presidential versus parliamentary systems, federal versus unitary states, direct versus indirect elections – is intended to allow the smooth functioning of the state and to guarantee that democracy's first principle, that the people alone are sovereign, is sustained.

The principle of citizen sovereignty is primary because we know of no other way to ensure that government remains accountable to society's interests rather than purely its own. This does not mean that a monarchy, autocracy or even a dictatorship cannot for a time produce the same policies as a democracy or that it cannot produce those policies more efficiently. History is replete with examples of benevolent dictators who have advanced their societies in useful ways. But no one has developed a way to ensure benevolence or even the competence of the autocrat. Democracy is but a modest human invention, albeit one replete with human frailties, that seeks to resolve this dilemma of leadership.

The resolution of this dilemma, however, places a strain on newly formed democratic institutions that frequently makes it appear as though democratic process is the least useful one to achieve specific results such as economic transformation and the realization of political stability. But efficiency and stability are not our only goals. We also seek a government that abides by several important normative principles, including the ideas that 'all men are created equal' and that 'each person is endowed with the right to life, liberty and justice'. These principles place constraints on the state that rarely apply even to the benevolent despot and which cause democracy itself to function in ways that sometimes seem less than perfect.

The dilemma of democracy is not the sacrifice of efficiency and stability, but that of combining the principles of citizen sovereignty and equality so as to ensure the protection of everyone's rights, including those of minorities against majorities. The dilemma of democracy, then, is finding ways to give both the majority and minority their rights simultaneously. In what might otherwise appear to be an unresolvable contradiction, we must decide when the majority ought to rule and when the minority should prevail, and then we must design institutions that guarantee outcomes that meet these constraints. So in asking whether we can be a democracy, we should not look simply at economic issues or at the prospects for peaceful transitions of power. We must ask whether we can envision political institutions that allow for the gradual realization of rights on everyone's part, because:

> *Rule 53*: A 'democratic' state cannot be stable for long if some minority cannot realize its rights; and if such a state is stable, then it cannot be a democracy.

Minimally, then, we must accept the idea that minorities ought to be protected when their interests are intense and when those of the majority are weak. The difficulty, however, is that we have no simple way to measure intensity. Thus we cannot ask how much a person is willing to pay for, say, freedom of speech – we simply grant that right to everyone. But mere words cannot ensure anything – rights are ensured only through the operation of institutions. Unfortunately, the principle of citizen sovereignty seems to dictate the application in one form or another of majority rule, which only returns us once again to the problem of protecting minority rights against majority tyranny. But there is a solution: eschew simplistic conceptualizations of democratic process – policy chosen by referenda, laws passed by a single legislative body, decrees issued by an otherwise unrestrained popularly elected president. Instead we require that to change a policy or to initiate a new one, a majority must sustain itself through a complex array of institutional hurdles. It must first elect a majority of representatives (usually to each of two legislative chambers); it must form a majority in each legislative chamber, if not in various subcommittees of the legislature; it must elect a president who will sustain this legislation without a veto; and that legislation must be deemed constitutional by a majority of members of some court that oversees the constitutionality of legislation. Each of these stages gives minorities the opportunity to block changes in the status quo that threaten their interests or violate their rights.

Creating a democracy, then, requires the design and implementation of institutions – legislative ones, electoral ones, judicial ones and even bureaucratic ones – where those institutions 'fit together' not only to protect individual rights but also to form a coherent state. It follows, then, that states making a transition to democracy cannot be content with some incomplete or simplified version of this form of governance. If democracy is to fulfil its full promise, it must be developed in its entirety. We cannot have merely a directly elected president or a newly elected legislature or newly appointed court. We must have all things simultaneously.

Admittedly, because it imposes a requirement on itself that despots and autocrats need not meet – that policies opposed by minorities progress through numerous hurdles before they are accepted – democracy often seems incapable of making definitive and timely choices. The temptation will be great to short-circuit democratic process in favour of expediency. But we have at least two facts to support the argument that people should sustain the course of democratic transition, however uncomfortable that might seem on occasion. First, democracies have survived, and even prospered, through eras no less trying than the one confronting the successor states of the Soviet empire. Second, when called upon to make the right moral choice, democracies have done so even though majorities initially opposed such decisions. Democratic process has not always worked perfectly and its record is not unassailable. But on average, it has worked better than the alternatives.

Bibliography

Aranson, Peter H. (1990), 'Federalism', *Cato Journal*, **10** (1), 1–15.

Bogdanor, Vernon and David Butler (eds) (1983), *Democracy and Elections*, Cambridge: Cambridge University Press.

Chandler, William M. (1987), 'Federalism and political parties', in H. Bakvis and W.M. Chandler (eds), *Federalism and the Role of the State*, Toronto: University of Toronto Press.

Dahl, Robert A. (1956), *A Preface to Democratic Theory*, New Haven: Yale University Press.

Dahl, Robert A. (1989), *Democracy and its Critics*, New Haven: Yale University Press.

Di Palma, Giuseppe (1990), *To Craft Democracies: An Essay on Democratic Transitions*, Berkeley: University of California Press.

Diamond, Larry and Marc F. Plattner (eds) (1993), *The Global Resurgence of Democracy*, Baltimore: Johns Hopkins University Press.

Diamond, Larry and Marc F. Plattner (eds) (1994), *Nationalism, Ethnic Conflict, and Democracy*, Baltimore: Johns Hopkins University Press.

Duverger, Maurice (1954), *Political Parties: Their Organization and Activity in the Modern State*, New York: Wiley.

Elster, Jon (1989), *The Cement of Society*, Cambridge: Cambridge University Press.

Elster, Jon and Rune Slagstad (eds) (1988), *Constitutionalism and Democracy*, Cambridge: Cambridge University Press.

Foley, Michael (1990), *The Silence of Constitutions*, New York: Routledge.

Grofman, Bernard (ed.) (1993), *Information, Participation, and Choice*, Ann Arbor: University of Michigan Press.

Grofman, Bernard and Arend Lijphart (eds) (1986), *Electoral Laws and their Political Consequences*, New York: Agathon Press.

Hardin, Russell (1989), 'Why a constitution', in B. Grofman and D. Wittman (eds), *The Federalist Papers and the New Institutionalism*, New York: Agathon Press.

Hermens, F.A. (1972), *Democracy or Anarchy: A Study of Proportional Representation*, 2nd edition, New York: Johnson Reprint Corp.

Hoag, C.G. and G.C. Hallett, Jr (1926), *Proportional Representation*, New York: Macmillan.

Horowitz, Donald (1985), *Ethnic Groups in Conflict*, Berkeley: University of California Press.

Horowitz, Donald (1991), *A Democratic South Africa: Constitutional Engineering in a Divided Society*, Berkeley: University of California Press.

Jones, Mark P. (1993), 'The political consequences of electoral laws in Latin America and the Caribbean', *Electoral Studies,* **12** (1), 59–75.

Lemco, Jonathan (1991), *Political Stability in Federal Governments*, New York: Praeger.

Lewis, David (1969), *Convention*, Cambridge: Harvard University Press.

Lijphart, Arend (1984), *Democracies*, New Haven: Yale University Press.

Lijphart, Arend (ed.) (1992), *Parliamentary versus Presidential Government*, Oxford: Oxford University Press.

Lijphart, Arend and Bernard Grofman (eds) (1984), *Choosing an Electoral System*, New York: Praeger.

Linz, Juan J. (1990), 'The perils of presidentialism', *Journal of Democracy*, **1**, Winter, 51–69.

Linz, Juan J. and Arturo Valenzuela (1994), *The Failure of Presidential Democracy*, Baltimore: Johns Hopkins University Press.

Mainwaring, Scott (1990), 'Presidentialism in Latin America', *Latin American Review*, **25**, 157–79.

Mainwaring, Scott (1993), 'Presidentialism, multipartism and democracy', *Comparative Political Studies*, **26** (2), 28–50.

Olson, Mancur (1965), *The Logic of Collective Action*, Cambridge: Harvard University Press.

Olson, Mancur (1982), *The Rise and Decline of Nations*, New Haven: Yale University Press.

Ordeshook, Peter C. (1993), 'Some rules of constitutional design', in E.F. Paul, F.D. Miller and J. Paul (eds), *Liberalism and the Economic Order*, Cambridge: Cambridge University Press.

Ordeshook, Peter C. (1995), 'Institutions and incentive: the prospects for Russian democracy', *Journal of Democracy*, **6**, April, 46–60.

Ordeshook, Peter C. and Olga Shvetsova (1995), 'If Madison and Hamilton were merely lucky, what hope is there for Russian Federalism', *Constitutional Political Economy*, **6** (2), 107–27.

Ostrom, Vincent (1991), *The Meaning of American Federalism*, San Francisco: ICS Press.

Popkin, Samuel (1991), *The Reasoning Voter: Communication and Persuasion in Presidential Campaigns*, Chicago: University of Chicago Press.

Rabushka, Alvin and Kenneth Shepsle (1972), *Politics in Plural Societies*, Columbus, Ohio: Merrill Publishing.

Rae, Douglas (1967), *The Political Consequences of Electoral Laws*, New Haven: Yale University Press.

Riker, William H. (1964), *Federalism: Origin, Operation, Significance*, Boston: Little Brown.

Riker, William H. (1982), *Liberalism and the Democratic Order*, Prospect Heights, Illinois: Waveland Press.

Riker, William H. (ed.) (1987), *The Development of American Federalism*, Boston: Kluwer Academic Publishers.

Rossiter, Clinton (ed.) (1961), *The Federalist Papers*, New York: Bantam Books.

Rowe, Nicholas (1989), *Rules and Institutions*, Ann Arbor: University of Michigan Press.

Sartori, Giovanni (1994), *Comparative Constitutional Engineering*, New York: New York University Press.

Schattschneider, E.E. (1960), *A Realist's View of Democracy in America*, Hinsdale, Illinois: Dryden.

Schmitt, Carl (1985), *The Crisis of Parliamentary Democracy*, translated by Ellen Kennedy, Cambridge: MIT Press.

Schwartz, Thomas (1989), 'Publius and public choice', in B. Grofman and D. Wittman (eds), *The Federalist Papers and the New Institutionalism*, New York: Agathon Press.

Scully, Gerald W. (1992), *Constitutional Environment and Economic Growth*, Princeton: Princeton University Press.

Shugart, Matthew S. and John M. Carey (1992), *Presidents and Assemblies: Constitutional Design and Electoral Dynamics*, New York: Cambridge University Press.

Sundquist, James L. (1992), *Constitutional Reform and Effective Government*, Washington, DC: The Brookings Institute.

Sunstein, Cass M. (1990), 'Constitutionalism, prosperity, democracy', *Constitutional Political Economy*, **2** (3), 371–94.

Taagepera, Rein and Matthew S. Shugart (1989), *Seats and Votes: The Effects and Determinants of Electoral Systems*, New Haven: Yale University Press.

Wagner, Richard E. (1993), *Parchment, Guns and Constitutional Order*, Brookfield, VT: Elgar Publishing.
Wallich, Christine I. (ed) (1994), *Russia and the Challenges of Fiscal Federalism*, Washington, DC: World Bank.

Index

abstention from voting, 30
abuse of power, 54, 103–4
accommodation, 39–40
activism, 10–13
ambiguity, 54
America's Association for Retired
    People (AARP), 11
Argentina, 37
aspirations, 45
assembly: right of, 46–7
asymmetric federalism, 71
authoritarian state, 38
autonomy, regional, 71–2, 76–7, 116,
    117, 123

balance of power, 60–62, 105
Baltic states, 1
Belarus, 123
Belgium, 122
beliefs, 54–5
bilateral negotiation, 116
Bolivar, S., 101
Britain, 2, 93

campaign financing, 17, 31–2
Canada, 70, 76, 94, 122
Central Election Commission, 117
central government see national
    government
centralization, 72–3
challenger, need for a, 30
Chile, 36
China, 36, 37, 69, 103
citizens
    enforcement of constitution, 65
    lists of obligations, 44–5
    qualities needed for democracy, 8–
        14
    relationship of state to, 59–60

sovereignty, 12–13, 46–7, 124–5
civil war, 79–80
cleavages, 32–3, 98–9
coalitions, 79–80
    instability, 33–4, 98
coercion, 30
collective action, 10–13
communism, 14, 52
Communist Party, 57–8, 60
competition
    local political, 21
    national-regional, 70–71
competitive elections see elections
conflict
    regional conflicts, 72–3
    society's inherent conflicts, 5–6
consensus, 52–3
consistency, 54
constitution, 78, 123
    emergency clauses, 103–10
    enforcement, 65–6
    expectations and importance of
        new, 56–62
    and legislature, 86–8
    and legitimization, 57–8
    norm-creation, 51–2
    resolving society's inherent
        conflicts, 5–6
    rules for writing, 63–8
    Russia, 61, 89, 113–14, 123
    supremacy of federal law, 73–4
constitutional rights, 43–9, 67–8
contracts, 73
co-optation, 20–21
coordination of the state, 107–8
corruption, 109–10
Costa Rica, 119
crime, 109–10
'crisis of norms', 51

cross-cutting interests, 32–3
Czechoslovakia, 101

decree, 39, 84
defence, 73
democracy, 1–7
    communism and, 14
    failings of incomplete, 39–41
    feasibility in Central and Eastern
        Europe, 121–6
    role of voting, 25–6
    rules of design, 4–6
Democratic Party (US), 20, 78–9, 82,
    88
despotism, enlightened, 36–7
disasters, natural, 104–5
discrimination, 47
Duma, 89, 116
    elections, 115, 117–18, 119
duties, citizens', 44–5

economic problems, 70–71, 104,
    106–7
economic reform: and political
    reform, 35–42, 111–12
election rules, 86–8, 118–20, 123
    parliamentary, 101–2, 115, 117–
        20
    presidential, 87–8, 100–102, 114–
        15, 118–20
    two-chamber legislature, 93–5
elections
    citizen sovereignty, 12
    constitutional rights and, 47
    fair and competitive, 28–34
    incentive for legislature, 84–8
    local and regional, 81–2
    political parties, 79–82, 85, 87–8
    scheduling, 31
    turnout, 30–31, 101
    see also voters; voting
emergency clauses, 103–10
enforcement of constitution, 65–6
enlightened despotism, 36–7
entry, 29–30
environment, 73
Estonia, 122
ethnicity, 19–21, 33, 80, 91–2

European Community, 70
executive
    conflict with legislature, 97, 100,
        101–2
    legislature, judiciary and, 48–9,
        59–61
extra-constitutional organizations,
    10–13
extremists, 16–17, 29

fairness, 91–2
    competitive elections, 28–34
    institutions, 54–5
fascism, 123
federal law: supremacy of, 74
Federal Treaty, 116
federalism, 48, 69–75
    political parties and, 76–82
    Russia's choices, 113, 115–18
Federation Council, 89, 116–17
Finland, 91
Franklin, B., 112
fraud, vote, 31
free press, 12, 30
fundamental rights *see* constitutional
    rights

Germany, 7, 40, 94, 98
Gorbachev, M.S., 22
governmental structure, 47–9, 59–62
    see also state
grievances, redress of, 47

Hitler, A., 40
Hungary, 91, 98

Iceland, 91
ignorance, 40–41
incentives, 5, 112–13, 114, 120
    legislators, 84, 117–18
'incompetents', 29
information, political, 9–11, 16
    sources for voters, 17
institutions, 4–5, 123, 125–6
    constitution and, 47–8, 67–8
        appropriateness, 57–8
    influence of democratic, 50–55
    participatory organizations, 10–13

political institutional development, 37–8
insurrection, 104, 106
interests
  cross-cutting, 32–3
  in newly-formed democracies, 39
internal checks and balances, 54, 103–4, 105
internal security agencies, 109
invasion, 104–5
Israel, 98
issues, policy, 30, 67–8
Italy, 122

Japan, 7, 36, 37, 123
Jefferson, T., 73
judiciary
  and corruption, 109–10
  relationship to executive and legislature, 48–9, 59–61

King, M. Luther, 20
Korea, South, 36, 37
Kuomingtang Party (Korea), 37

language
  in constitution, 45–6, 66–7
  of democracy, 3
Latin America, 48
Latvia, 122
law
  due process of, 46–7
  supremacy of federal, 74
leaders, political, 6, 124
  citizen sovereignty, 12–13
  incentives and constitutional rights, 47–9
  legislative efficiency, 83–8
  referenda and, 26–7
  role of voting in a democracy, 25–6
learning, political *see* information
legislative districts, 93–5
legislature, 83–8
  conflict with executive, 97, 100, 101–2
  relationship to judiciary and executive, 48–9, 59–61
  two-chamber, 89–96
legitimization: constitution and, 57–8
local elections, 81–2
local government, 41, 123
local political competition, 21
losing and winning, 33–4
Lubell, S., 82

Madison, J., 7, 47, 52, 61–2, 112
  clash of interests, 32
  separation of powers, 100
majority rule, 20, 125
  popular will and, 23–4
  two-chamber legislature, 93–5
majority with run-off election procedure, 100–101, 118, 119
mandate, 101–2, 114–15
Mau, V., 118
media, 12, 30
military dictatorship, 35–6
minorities, 20–21
  protecting rights of, 93–5, 124–5
money
  election campaigns, 17, 31–2
  supply, 73

national government
  conflict with regional governments, 70–71
  functions in federalism, 72, 73–4
nationalism, 19–21
  see also ethnicity
natural disasters, 104–5
Nigeria, 69, 70, 101
norms, social 50–51, 66–8
  see also rules

obligations, citizens', 44–5

parliament: president's relations with, 113–15
parliamentary elections, 101–2, 115, 117–20
parliamentary systems, 18–19, 60, 80–81
  and presidential systems, 97–102
participatory organizations, 10–13
party labels, 18, 82, 85

see also political parties
People's Congress, 22, 84, 97, 108, 114, 116
personal experiences, 17
pessimism, 56–7
policy issues, 30, 67–8
political information *see* information
political leaders *see* leaders, political
political parties, 85
  and election rules, 86–8
  in a federation, 76–82
  and PR, 98–9
  Russia's choices, 113, 118
  USA, 77–82, 117
  voters and, 17–21
political reform, 111–13, 119–20
  and economic reform, 35–42, 111–12
popular referenda, 22–7
popular will, 23–6
power
  abuse of, 54, 103–4
  balance of, 60–62, 105
preferences, 25–6
preparation, 40–41
president/presidency
  emergencies, 108
  relations with parliament, 113, 113–15
  strength of, 3
presidential elections, 79–80, 100–102
  rules in Russia, 114–15, 118–20
  rules in USA, 87–8
presidential systems, 18–19, 60
  crime and corruption, 109
  and parliamentary systems, 97–102
  USA, 78–81
press freedom, 12, 30
privatization, 41
property rights, 37–8, 41–2, 46–7
proportional representation (PR), 19, 93
  election to Duma, 115, 118, 119
  parliamentary systems and presidential systems, 98–9, 101–2

qualifications, constitutional, 46, 54

redress of grievances, 47
referenda, 22–7
regional autonomy, 71–2, 76–7, 116, 117, 123
regional conflicts, 72–3
regional elections, 81–2
regional government, 74, 123
  see also federalism
regional-national conflict, 70–71
regions: representation and, 91–2
religious freedom, 46–7
representation
  legislature and, 86–8, 91–2
  voting in a democracy, 25–6
Republican Party (US), 20, 78–9, 88
responsibilities, citizens', 44–5
revolutions, 51–2
rights, 122–3
  constitutional, 43–9, 67–8
  dilemma of democracy, 124–5
  emergencies and, 105
  property rights, 37–8, 41–2, 46–7
  protecting minority rights, 93–5, 124–5
Romania, 99
Roosevelt, F.D., 82
rules, 3, 4, 61–2
  influence of democratic institutions, 50–55
  for writing constitutions, 63–8
Russia, 1, 31, 80, 91, 98
  choices, 111–20
    federal relations, 115–18
    political parties, 118
    presidential-parliamentary relations, 113–15
    reform, 119–20
  constitution, 61, 89, 113–14, 123
  emergency, 108, 109
  extremism, 16–17
  legislature, 83, 84
    two-chamber, 89, 94
  referendum, 22

scheduling of elections, 31
secession, 20–21

security agencies, internal, 109
self-interest, 52–3
   legislature, 85–6, 117
   political reform and, 111–12, 120
self-rule, 63–4
separation of powers, 48, 60, 100
Shumieko, V., 118
social norms, 50–51, 66–8
   see also rules
sovereign states, 116
sovereignty, citizen, 12–13, 46–7,
   124–5
Soviet Union
   constitutions, 56–8, 63
   dissolution, 70
   voting, 28
speech, free, 46–7
state, 43
   authoritarian, 38
   coordination of, 107–8
   sovereign's agent, 46–7
   structure, 47–9, 59–62
Sumner, C., 83
supremacy of federal law, 74
Switzerland, 26, 70, 77, 101
symmetrical federalism, 71–2

Taiwan, 36, 37, 41, 83, 103
temporary dictator, 84, 106–7
terms of office, 95
Tocqueville, A. de, 41
trade, 73
turnout, election, 30–31, 101
two-chamber legislature, 89–96
two-party system, 87–8

Ukraine, 1, 80, 91, 99
United States (USA), 2, 77, 123

AARP, 11
civil rights movement, 20
Civil War, 70
constitutional rights ignored, 48
federalism, 77–82, 117, 121–2
inherent conflicts and constitution,
   6
local elections, 27
political parties, 77–82, 117
presidential election rules, 87–8
privatization, 41–2
self-interest, 112
separation of powers, 100
strength of the presidency, 3
two-chamber legislature, 92, 94
violence in Congress, 83
Uzbeckistan, 1

values, 52
violence, 20–21
vote fraud, 31
voters, 15–21
voting, 30
   popular referenda, 22–7
   see also elections
Vyshinsky, A., 28

will, popular, 23–6
winning and losing, 33–4

Yeltsin, B., 16, 22, 31, 109, 117,
   122
   1993 draft constitution, 116
   and People's Congress, 84, 97,
      108, 114, 116
Yugoslavia, 69, 70

Zhirinovsky, V., 16, 31, 115